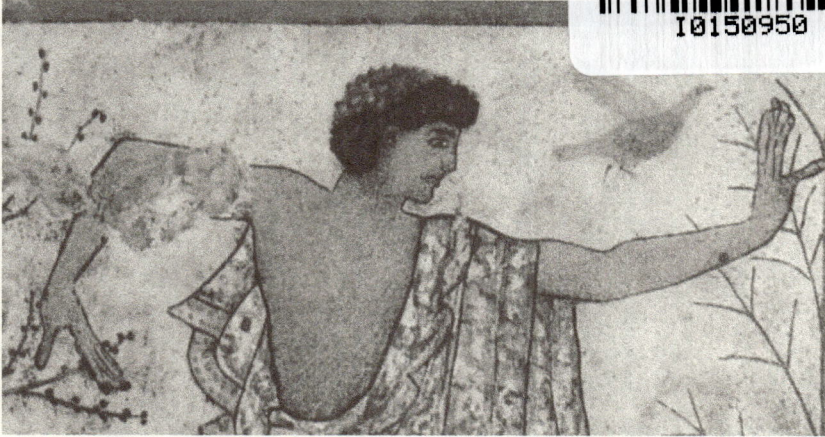

THE DANCE
THAT BEGINS
AND BEGINS

SELECTED POEMS
1973-2013

by
JACK VEASEY

The Poet's
Press
PITTSBURGH, PA

ISBN 0-922558-78-7
Also available as a PDF ebook

This is the 211th publication of
THE POET'S PRESS
2209 Murray Avenue #3
Pittsburgh, PA 15217

PRAISE FOR JACK VEASEY'S EARLIER WORK

A true poet. — Rita Mae Brown

Jack Veasey's poems mourning his father are unique in modern poetry — and welcome, for the absence of the usual father-son problems, honoring, instead, his open-hearted grief. Perhaps it is because of this that Jack Veasey emerges from these poems as a man firmly rooted in the earth from which he sprang ... powerful. — Edward Field

My own belief is that any writer who writes one line I can't forget is a poet. Jack Veasey, in his wonderful scope, goes deep into his unexplored personal mines. His grasp of form, image and language are graceful and true. His revelations and discoveries are gifts to the reader. And the lines! There are so many. How they gleam! Damn good stuff. — Eric Blau

Jack Veasey's poetry comes like a shaft of cold air into a stuffy room.
— Barbara A. Holland

PRESS ACCLAIM FOR JACK VEASEY'S RECENT BOOK, *SHAPELY*

The poet laureate has to be able to relate to many different types of people, from grassroots bohemians to the Union League bowtie-wearing crowd. It's too bad that the Fishtown-born poet Jack Veasey is now a Harrisburg native. Veasey would make a good Philadelphia poet laureate. — Thom Nickels, *The Huffington Post*

Poet Jack Veasey writes stories — hard, nitty-gritty, ironic, heartfelt stories. Many of Veasey's poems exhibit his struggle of growing up gay in the tough Fishtown neighborhood of Philadelphia, where Archie Bunker types ruled and where the nuns in his Catholic school were tougher than old meat. It also didn't help that Veasey had the attitudes and values of a hippie in this place and at this time. "The neighborhood's old atmosphere still pervades a lot of my work. It gave me an outsider's perspective and made me identify with the underdog. That colors a lot of my choices of subjects, and the viewpoints from which I write, even when they aren't my own. Poetry is my life," Veasey muses. "I continue to write for pretty much the same reason as I continue to breathe." The narrative poems relay that yearning, the pangs, the loss. "It's how I make sense of being in the world." — Lori M. Myers, *The Burg*, Harrisburg, PA

TABLE OF CONTENTS

PREFACE

My intention with this collection of poems – though its subtitle is "Selected Poems 1973-2013," and the poems in it are drawn from that whole forty year period of time — is not so much to offer up a general Selected Poems book as to tell the story of my life and psyche up to this point. As a gay man born in the middle of the repressive 1950s to working class Irish Catholic parents in a rough inner city American East Coast neighborhood — and who came of age in the wild 1970s — I've had a lot of vivid, often difficult, experience to process. I find myself with things to say about relationships, politics, sexuality, spirituality, and other subjects. But I couldn't really organize these poems chronologically in a way that would effectively tell my story and convey my meanings.

Instead, I've organized the poems into sections that deal with particular "territory" I've covered — certain kinds of experiences and relationships I've had, and of things I've witnessed, that were common to folks like me in my time and place, and in some cases still are. The section titles give strong clues as to the nature of these experiences and situations. You could say the sections are "thematic," but that's a bit more general than what I really mean. In some cases, poems grouped in the same section may be set in very different places and periods of time. The poems themselves are mostly linear; the order in which I've arranged them is not. Events of a particular type may have occurred repeatedly throughout my life, but their effects — the insights they gave me, the ways they've changed me — have been gradual and cumulative. The order of the poems reflects that psychic "timeline," not a literal chronology.

The first section, "Shaken Foundations," deals with growing up, young adulthood, family (including the conflicts common to many of us — and the deaths of family members that impact on us early in life). "Nuts And Bolts" explores sexuality and the gay subculture of the 1970s. "Distances" reflects on encounters with homophobia and religious bigotry. "Conditions" reflects on my changing environments — urban and then, later in life, small town and rural experiences — and things I've witnessed in both circumstances. "Sideshow" observes culture, from mythology to films and comic books. Finally, "That Evening Sun" comes from a mature perspective, examining such things as struggles with health issues, the passing of friends, the comforts and difficulties of long-term domestic life, and even, eventually, epiphanies that I'd call spiritual, for want of a better term. This last section's title seems familiar because it comes from the lyrics of the classic song "St. Louis Blues." It's also the title of my favorite William Faulkner story.

Also: about my use of the second person — when I address a poem to "You," it is not necessarily a poem written to my life partner. These poems are drawn from a long period of time, and many of them deal with people and experiences from the distant past. There are also times when I address a poem to a "You" when I am, in fact, talking to myself.

I haven't included notes on individual poems this time because my poems in this collection are mostly fairly straightforward narratives.

— Jack Veasey

THE DANCE
THAT BEGINS
AND BEGINS

*This collection is dedicated to my partner in life,
the sweet and saintly David Walker, with all my love.*

SHAKEN FOUNDATIONS

A CHILD'S GOD

They leave him
and turn out the lights.
He is not tired, but they tell him
it's time
to sleep.

When he closes his eyes,
a square of pale green light
appears, right
at the center of
that blackness
that is always there
when he closes his eyes.
For a moment, he has
a green night-light,
relieving the dark
of the room beyond
his eyelids.
But he can't hold the green glow
in his view;
it fades, as does
the trail of red sparks
that remain
with him a half-second longer.
Then there is only
the dark,
and whatever it holds.

<3>

What is this dark?
Is it nothing?
Is it just
the absence of light?
Or is it a place
in which things hide
and wait,
and when he falls asleep
they'll show themselves,
come out to play those dramas
they call "dreams?"

This little boy
wants to know.
And so,
in the dark,
he asks God.
But the boy gets
no answer.
And still, he refuses to think
he is in here alone;

because he is afraid of the dark;

and, if he is afraid,
there must be something there.

<4>

MR. MARTIN

Mr. Martin was my high school typing teacher
at an all-boy Catholic school.
He was also the first man I ever loved.

Right after last period,
I'd stop by to see him before I left school.
It never occurred to me
that anybody else
might think this strange.
I'd babble about nothing
while he wiped the writing
off the chalk board, banged erasers,
put the plastic cover
over each machine.

I never wondered
what he thought of
my devotion. Everyone I knew,
my family included,
treated me as if
the notion that I might have any feelings
was unthinkable. I just expected him
to do the same. I never imagined
the pangs I felt
showed in my eyes.

He wasn't a big man.
His cheeks turned bluish
in the afternoon
from stubble whose replenishment
impressed me. He wore his short black hair

<5>

slicked down, smelled like
a cigarette, rolled back
his white shirt sleeves.
He'd often stand
and watch his students pound away
with forearms crossed
over his chest. I never thought
he saw me watching him.
When he'd bark
instructions at us,
it would always strike me
that he sounded like
a gangster on TV.

Of course, the other kids in class
raised the first questions
in the cruelest way they could.
One asked him to say
that he would see me later
in the locker room,
and, thick head that he was,
he did, in front of all of them.
I felt as though
he'd slapped me. He could tell
something was wrong,
but it took him awhile
to figure out exactly what.

When he got married,
I went through several reactions,
and they puzzled even me.
I could discuss them
with no one.
I felt like I was losing

<6>

my connection with him,
though I'd still see him
each day. I was hurt
he didn't ask me to the wedding.
I wished I could show him
I was happy for him, though
that wasn't quite the truth.
I felt like I should give him a present,
though, thank God, I didn't.

I had a girlfriend, too,
though mine was a "beard," as they say,
that I was using
to delude myself.
When she (wisely) broke it off with me,
I panicked. I even swore out loud
in front of Mr. Martin.
He objected to
my language — he'd already
started distancing himself —
and told me not
to come to see him anymore.

I stayed home from school
the next day, claiming
that I was sick.
I was amazed
when the phone rang,
and it was him.

He asked why I wasn't in school.
I repeated my lie.
He said, with anger,
"What about tomorrow,

<7>

and the next day,
and the next?"
I heard myself blurt out,
"I didn't think you'd care"
And then he answered,
"Well, I do."

I went back to school
The next day — though, from then on,
I'd only visit him
on rare occasions.
When our eyes met,
it was awkward.

I began to live my life
outside of school — outside
even my dreams.
I began to do things
I'd denied I even
thought about.
I learned that love can hurt you
even worse
when it's expressed, even
returned. Eventually, I left
high school
and home.

As for Mr. Martin,
I have no idea
if he's still alive,
although he gave me
my first evidence
that I was.

<8>

There's a proverb:
to learn a thing,
teach it.
Yet, even if
you teach a thing
by accident,
the lesson
will be clear.

Chalk dust in the air,
transient white words
on a black background —
a contrast
perhaps a bit too obvious,
just waiting
to be wiped away.

Through the chalky lens of memory
I picture Mr. Ryan,
my high school English teacher —
a little man in tweed
and granny glasses.
He had two lists of books:
one that he showed the priests,
one only we would see.
We could pick what books we'd read
from either list.
I picked D.H. Lawrence,
and it changed my life.
The two male friends
who wrestled naked

<9>

in *Women In Love*
opened my mind
to many possibilities.

Decades later, I heard
that, when told I was gay,
Mr. Ryan remarked,
"I knew the kid had problems,
but I didn't think that
that was one of them."

Sometimes we don't know
what we teach.
They clap the erasers together
and tell us to write what appears
in the cloud. Later,
we chalk it all up
to experience.

<10>

...AND THEN CAME THE PLAGUE
OF FROGS

In the early 1970s,
in high school Biology lab,
Father Flaherty required that every boy
cut up a frog.
This was gross,
but it might not have been so bad
if the frogs had been dead already.

They were kept
refrigerated in flat boxes
that looked like
they should hold pizza.
They'd been chloroformed,
or something. The cold
slowed down body processes,
and kept them in suspended animation.
"Your" frog would be laid out
spread-eagled on a board,
with pins stuck through its four webbed feet
to hold it down. You couldn't help
but notice the resemblance
to a crucifixion. Did I mention
this was Catholic school,
where we were taught
abortion was against God's law
because "all life" was sacred?

<11>

We were told
that it was better
if the frogs were still alive,
so we could see the beating of their hearts.
Father Flaherty did not laugh
when I asked him,
"Couldn't I just take its pulse?"
And he was even less amused
when I refused to do it —
that is, take a scalpel
to a healthy living thing.
I was surprised
I was the only one who wouldn't.
I was not surprised
that he gave me detention.
I was just as glad that he sent me
immediately to the office of the principal —
I didn't want to see the gruesome exercise —
but on my way out, I lifted a scalpel.

After my detention,
when there were way fewer people
in the building, I went back and used the blade
to pick the lock to the lab door.
I had a plan, albeit it not
that well thought out.
No one would have to guess too hard
to figure out who did it.
But I didn't concern myself with consequences.
I was thinking of
the other frogs
still sleeping in flat boxes,
dreaming of warm ponds
and scrumptious crunchy bugs.

<12>

I would remove the boxes
from the fridge; leave them, lids open,
on the tables, leave
the doors open as well.

I wish now
that I'd taken the boxes outside
to give the frogs a fighting chance.
As it was, a lot of them
fell victim to the quite imaginative cruelty
of my rammy teenaged classmates
who, next morning, found them
hopping happily all through the halls
of that godawful school.

Yes, it was worth
getting suspended.

I may never have been
popular, but, for a few years later,
I'd be
legendary.

<13>

PILLOW TALK
(or SYMPATHETIC MAGIC)

My pillow is confused.
It's not used
to the front side of my head,
to slow, sensuous
kisses
and caresses.
It didn't know it had a name
that I could murmur into it.
It wonders what
that strange new
wetness is
sometimes.

Worse, now it feels
pangs of its own.
It lies awake
and counts the hours till bedtime,
lonely for its owner
(just as he is
for his).

I think about investing it
with magic;
maybe a lock of your hair
in the pillowcase,
maybe a few
incantations.
Then, no matter
where you might be in your travels —
many miles from me, and even your mind

<14>

elsewhere —
when I wrap my arms around you
you might feel it,
you might think of me
and sense my longing,
long for me
a little
too.

<15>

AFTER THE LAST MORNING AFTER (1984)

Eddie's dead.
His hard night hit him too hard,
or, perhaps, he'd had enough

of stumbling, drunken,
through the dance-floor's
flashing
thunder, snorting
poppers, popping
pills, perusing
all the other
unpursue-ables.

Because he was nineteen
and almost pretty
in his pale, lean, half-
crazed way, because
his brittle little laugh
cracked loudest, keeping questions
all at bay, because
he gave away,
on darker days,
what some would trade
for pay, because
he drew a lucid music
from raw rudeness
and real wisdom from
one-liners, and knew

<16>

where
and how
and when to
wear
those
clothes,

because he paid the cost of chaos
and kept going,
we assumed
he really knew
what he was doing;
we assumed
he'd just passed out
and not passed
on (left on the landing
covered roughly with
a blanket, safe
since we had lugged him
home.) He *had* been
cold, but being cold
was Eddie's way.

We had been through this
with him
a hundred times —

and, when the midday came,
he'd always waken, white
as bone, blood-
shot, and groan
from his sick stomach
and hurt head.

<17>

This time, there were two differences:
he didn't wake,
and worse,
we couldn't blame him (though
we also couldn't bear to blame
ourselves)

Because
he wore the brash mask
of a bad boy, got it up
and gave good head, no matter
what stuff spiked his mind,
because
of all the blinding things he did
and all the stinging little things
he said, we thought
he knew what he was doing,
knew the way back
and would wake
as on so many other whacked-out mornings
when the leaky popper in his pocket
filled the room with fumes
and we woke,
choking.

But Eddie's dead,
and chemicals can't cure him
of this final crashing
come-down.

I forget things
when my battered brain's
been sealed off
from the hungry world

<18>

I live in, colored
by a drugged abundance,

but I remember
Eddie, slouched
in shadow, staring
past the strobe-struck
dancers, staring
far beyond the bar-room
that became his universe
of youth and beauty
by way of a flashing light;
looking farther off
than in his normal
hardened pose, as if
his place were then
another
altogether.
I remember catching glimpses
of the look he always wore
in those rare moments, when
his thick defenses dropped
because he really thought
nobody else was looking.
His look

looked like a look
I think I sometimes wear
myself, when
I am trying, staring
silently and straining, dazed
but trying nonetheless,
when I am trying

<19>

to imagine
happiness.

What he was thinking
in such moments, no-one asked,
and now it's anybody's guess
as to who that lost boy was
or what he thought, or
what he felt, or even
wanted.
Sometimes,
in a single flash
of strobe
that frames the dance-floor
like a snapshot,
I could swear
I see his face,
and the face I see
is wearing that same look
of vacant eyes
and naked need —

but Eddie looked so much
like many people,
and the face
is a mistake.

<20>

AN INEVITABLE INSIGHT

For my 30th birthday, 4/4/1985

I saw Ron tonight on the subway —
first time in nine years.
With him were his strapping teenage sons.
They were laughing, heading
for some ballgame, for some place
where I would not know who to root for
(being not preoccupied enough
with power politics, and also
too distracted by male beauty).

Both sons are beautiful
now that they look like their father.

I remember the canoe trip
with the four of us, when Ron and I
were lovers, shortly after his divorce
and not so long before our break-up,
when we drifted off on different trips
and joined each other's missing person's lists —
I in his past mind, he in mine.

But, back then, both sons
had accepted me, their father's "funny" friend,
a scrawny kid
whose hands had always talked too much,
whose hair hung down below round shoulders,
so unlike their father's shoulders,
so bereft of
heft and brawn.

<21>

They had ignored
the obvious, and let the love go
where it went, not knowing
it would one day go away.
But anyway, we'd shared a lot that day,

so I was tempted
to call out, wave, make
eye contact, penetrate
their heady jargon of fond slaps
and gentle jostles.
But I brought myself
to do none of these things,
really not sure
they'd recognize me,

because those boys
are now the age I was
when Ron was more than memory to me,
when I was young enough
to feel young love
and love it. I let my lover go,
and I grew older,
but I never thought
they would; all things
are as we left them in our minds
until time tells us otherwise.
And so they got off, laughing,
at my stop, not having seen me,
and I didn't. I was simply
dazed, too much to move,
caught clinging
on another kind of ride,
too stunned to stand up

<22>

for another stop or two,
not nearly ready to remember
so much difference
and distance, or
to feel a sadness I had said
was dead, or to see those young men
I'd believed still children,
or to wonder whether
they remember me,

now that I see
my life, illuminated
but unmoving, like a station
standing still and
shrinking steadily,
receding
through a dingy window
as the distance
lengthens, left behind
the surging, roaring, blurred,
relentless forward rush of
this
grey
train.

<23>

My Mom and Dad
both married other people
briefly. In 1950,
five years before I was born,
they both got divorced.
Rose had deserted my father;
Walter subjected my mother
to "indignities against her person,"
as The Court put it. Walter took exception
to Mom's claims,
which didn't get him anywhere.

Mom and Dad married each other
that same year. I wonder
if their exes have outlived them.

I wish I could talk
to Mom's first husband.
I suspect she learned
a lot of moves from him
that she would later use on me.
"I don't blame you,'" I'd say.
"If it had been possible,
I would have divorced her myself."

But I guess I'm glad
that Walter drove my mom away;
their breakup spared me
from a guttural last name
it would have choked me to pronounce.
And the personal indignities

<24>

that Mom would rain on me
gave me a lot in common
with my harried father.
As for Rose, I guess she wanted
someone stronger.

None of us can know
just what has vanished
in the gap between
the things we want
and what we end up getting.

<25>

His eyes are watery.
Not such a surprise
since they're blue,
but they're also red
at the corners,
behind the thick glasses
with broken brown frames
held together at one side
by bunched Scotch tape.
His V-necked t-shirt
shows a chest
from which all hair
has disappeared.
His guard uniform,
long unworn,
hangs cattycorner from him
on the outside
of the closet door.

He sits sunken
in his yellow-green
stuffed chair,
his black and white cat
sacked out
on the back of it,
fretfully wincing in
a twitchy dream.
Old books line the shelves
built in the wall beside him,
an assortment of odd titles:
ancient *Advice From Heloise*,

<26>

World War II Chronicles,
collected crossword puzzles,
and *Essays of Bishop Sheen*.
From the left arm of his chair
there hangs the cord,
with red light, of
a heating pad. His wife
will have to watch in case
it starts to smoke, or so
she likes to say.
Him, she no longer watches,
though he smokes a lot
these days; the doctor says,
"Just let him go. It's too late now."

He looks at, and past,
the TV where the blurry picture rolls,
for scenes he remembers
more vividly than the last hour.
His cousin the priest
will come later
to hear his confession,
as if he could commit a sin
just sitting here..

His son, who towers over him,
now knows
that hanging on
will hold him here;
he overheard
the hospice lady
tell him so.

<27>

He suspects this time will be
their final visit.

Like the doctor said,
"Just let him go."

<28>

MY FATHER'S FLAG

In a perfect triangle of plastic,
shut tight with a zipper,
sits a flag I won't unfold,
presented to my mother
at my father's grave
by a stiff stranger
in a soldier's uniform.

My mother fell apart
when he saluted her.
I had to hold her up,
though she, too
was a veteran
of other loved one's deaths.

When she died,
I got no flag
for her, despite
the fact that she spent
her whole life
at war
with everyone, her son
and self included.

But I would later find Dad's flag
buried in her house,
among the junk collected
for a lifetime. Now
it sits in my house,
still in plastic, thus
protected from the dust
that flakes from my own flesh.

<29>

I, too am at war,
if only with my past,
and I salute
the strange man in the mirror
who is some kind of survivor,
certainly.
His motto?
"Scars and stripes forever."

<30>

A VISIT TO YOUR MYSPACE PAGE

for Essra Mohawk

Last night, I listened
to your song
about your father.
It made me smile
sadly.

"He was always mad as hell," you said.
I remember.
you mentioned
how handsome he was.
I remember that, too:

dark skin
dark hair
dark eyes
dark spirit —
but fiery, always
still burning.

He told me once
that war
was natural,
just Nature's way
to shave off
excess population.

<31>

I told him I thought
that's why some people
were gay.
He huffed
and shrugged that off.

He always had to be right.
He had that in common
with you; that,
and a charm
that doggedly disarms
all but affection,
even when a rough edge
cuts.
Your philosophy, of course,
is just the opposite of his.

I noticed that I was
high on your friends list,
though I haven't been in touch
in much too long,
and I was moved.

How often I forget
what is important
to attend
to what is
merely pressing.

<32>

The passing of my own father
was one of many things
I thought might change that.

Then, I blinked;
years had gone by.

<33>

LUGGAGE

From this distance we can't see
the tightness of her grip —
this woman
whose hands are on the shoulders of the boy,
His back to us, his own hands clasped behind it.
The train station is nearly deserted,
a cavernous room that echoes every sound,
But we can't hear the words she's saying.
She's been talking a long time,
earnest and low. Neither she
nor the boy have moved a muscle;
he hasn't tried to get away;
whether he stays from fear, it's hard to tell.
Her words, inaudible; her face, unreadable,
she simply holds him there
and goes on talking.

"She must be his mother," you say;
Our train is late, and we began to watch
from boredom. But boredom quickly turns
to curiosity when there's a mystery involved.
I remind you that we haven't seen his face —
no way to check for a resemblance.
"I don't care if she *is* his mother,"
I hear myself say, suddenly
picturing my own. I know how tight
her grip would be; I know what tone of voice
her words would carry.

<34>

All this time kept waiting
till the train, the promised train,
takes me away, and still I won't move one inch further
from my mother, dead at last though she may be.
"I think she's hurting him," I say.
Yet we do nothing, knowing nothing
of the facts, which anyway
are not our business.

Loudly,
they announce our train;
we gather up our bags.
The woman goes on talking.
We begin to walk toward stairs
beyond which distant cities open
like new roses. But I take
one more look back.

<35>

WRITTEN AFTER DREAMING
OF MY MOTHER

My mother
has to catch
a train, dragging more baggage
than you'd think a car
could hold. The schedule says
it's leaving any minute.
She refuses
to let anybody help her,
and starts
cursing those who offer.

Ultimately, she will drag
her baggage down the tracks,
pulled on a rope
over her shoulder,
heading the wrong way,
aiming toward destinations
she just thinks she sees,
until the next train
runs her over.

I will wear her ashes
on my forehead,
crossed there by my cousin,
the Monsignor. In his head,
he'll carry her confession,
which blamed
everybody else.

<36>

In my head,
I carry
welts and scars
and always ranting
voices, the tracks of
my mother's passage.

And in my own passage
I trip
on scattered baggage,
strewn across
even my dreams.

<37>

MY MOTHER'S NEIGHBOR

Toward the end,
my mother's neighbor Phil
told me he knew
"All of the dirt"
about the "way
I'd treated her."
"She told me
everything," he said —
emphasis his —
"But I don't judge," adding this last
as if I should be grateful.

The truth was,
I'd bent over backwards
trying to be friends with her
as an adult,
though it meant
volunteering for abuse.

I was surprised
to hear he'd bought
her version of me.
He had often irritated me
with sneering stories of
her mental illness, even once
admitting that he'd hide
sometimes when she'd knocked
on his door.

<38>

Ironically, until that point,
I'd kept an open mind
about the man,
despite the mean things
Mom had said about him.

<39>

AFTERTASTE

Over dinner, you abruptly said
that your father was dead to you
already. It didn't much surprise me.

The waitress asked
if we would like drink refills.
We said yes.

Your father is now
in his 90s. He's been sick,
in the clinic unit
of the condo complex
you've described as
"Old People's Versailles" —
with its pools
and indoor park
of potted trees.

Back when he was in better health,
perhaps two years ago,
you sent him a letter
it took you a long time
to write — and it took a lot
besides time
out of you. You told him
how he'd hurt you
by refusing to accept you
as you are. He never
responded. Lately,
we haven't talked about him.
I have wondered
what was going on.

<40>

When he's dead, you say,
your sister
is the only family
you'll stay in touch with.

I don't find that
hard to understand.
Her husband, the smug preacher,
has long been an irritant
to both of us.
Your lovely late mother
I'd call a saint,
but visits with
some of the other
Christian fundamentalists
who share your blood
are awkward and polite, hinging
on which subjects
they and we
always leave out
of our conversation.

And my crazy mother
and my alcoholic father,
both gone now —
well, that's another
dark domestic story.

<41>

Sometimes blood is not just shared,
but *shed,*
to fit into a family,
when you cut off parts of yourself
to "keep the peace."

The coffee arrives.
You wonder aloud
whether this recent lack
of contact is your way
of preparing yourself
for his death, of somewhat blunting
any blow
you might still feel.
You don't know
if we should even
"do the funeral."

For a moment,
I flash back
To the last funeral
I had to "do,"
the one for my long-raging
mother, who you know
did not "go gentle
into that good night."
I was the one
who had to do
the burying, the smiling,
and the shaking hands
that time.

<42>

Nobody else was left
besides her hated sister,
who had made a scene
to try to force me
not to cremate,
though that had been
Mom's instruction.
She said Mom was trying to avoid
"the final Judgment,"
though the Church allowed the option.

At last, I'd had to point out
that, unfortunately, this
was not *her* funeral
we were discussing.
She'd missed my implication.

The chatter of the restaurant
continues, and the music
through the speakers,
the soft hits
from decades in our grown-up lives.
The waitress asks
if we will want
dessert.

We both say
yes, needing
some sweetness
to erase the taste
of things we have,
and haven't,
said.

<43>

Sun-hot cobblestones
remind me of the street
where Grand-pop Veasey lived
until he died. My uncle Skip,
poor lonely drunk, remained there
till his later death, which cleared the air
and let the house be sold.
The spoils were split
among too many hungry relatives,
our only shred of history torn loose.
No room on that street now
for such as we; the street was Elfreth's Alley,
long declared "historic"
and, at long last, all gentrified.

I wore my work boots
to his funeral,
and consequently got a sneer from my only male cousin,
who believed the myth
that his mom married "better,"
and that social climbing
could erase your roots.
But he'd still always be descended
from a long line of menial workers
on his mother's side,
the Irish side that gave him
the red hair and freckles
his aunts found so "cute."

<44>

I'd like to shove a work boot
up his ass, my foot
still in it —
little shit. Looking back, I don't know
what's become of him.

Some family connections
don't mean much. These days,
we've scattered over
younger asphalt streets
like ashes. That last fact
would have surprised us
once; like all good Catholics,
we buried our dead
in blessed soil.

<45>

We should wait till after dark, you said,
and I agreed.
I had gone there in the afternoon,
after she stopped breathing,
after we stopped crying
and holding on to each other
as we could not hold on to her.
On both sides of the bridge,
there were signs everywhere:
NO TRESPASSING.
PRIVATE PROPERTY.
VIOLATORS WILL BE ARRESTED.
And there was no place where you could walk
right to the edge of the water.
Neighbors we've never met
own every inch of the world
on that side of the tracks.

We passed the last house.
I led the way.
A camper was parked in the front yard,
not far from the river.
All its lights were on,
the canopy extended,
a card table and two lawn chairs
set outside, as if the occupants
would be right back.
Dogs barked somewhere
on the property
to warn them we were passing.
We would not want them

<46>

to notice us. Thank God
it would be darker
on the bridge.

You carried her
wrapped in a pink baby blanket.
The bridge curved uphill.
If it had been lighter,
you could have seen the water
through the slats under our feet. Cars hissed by us
with high beams on; one low stone wall
stood between us and them, another
between us and the river.
We were almost at the center,
at the top,
when an egret swooped over us —
only a yard or two above us, a huge black shadow
set against the sky's dim glow —
both of us gasped
at the sight and *whoosh!* sound.
We knew it meant something.
You told me later
that was when you knew
that everything would be all right.

You opened the blanket so we could see her,
touch her, say goodbye.
I stroked her fur, afraid she would feel stiff.
She didn't. She felt like herself,
though so utterly still.
She had lived with us seven years.

<47>

We couldn't afford a cremation.
There was no place private
we could bury her;
we rent our shred
of the town, and
we have no yard.
But we would give her
to the universe, to nature.
I told her that we loved her
and we always would, hoping
her spirit would hear me,
wherever it was.

We had decided that we'd keep
the blanket to remember her.
You let her drop.
It seemed the fall
took an impossibly long time.
Her small body
made a large splash.
We held each other
once more, wept again
for a few more minutes. Then
we turned away to take
the dark walk home.
And yes, I will confess
I did look back, searching
for that shadow in the sky.

<48>

NUTS AND BOLTS

PUBLIC PRIVACY

When you stare at a stranger
— unbeknownst to them —
before too long, they feel it.

They feel stalked, and turn
to check you out,
to meet your gaze.

You look away,
not wanting to invade —
OK, not wanting to get caught.

Sometimes you glimpse
their anger and suspicion —
a stranger's admiration

is not often welcome —
other times, they just
seem curious, giving you

just that much in common.
Either way, the contact
doesn't last; there is no time

for the unplanned
in modern life. And so,
unknown potential

passes by,
and fantasy
remains intact.

<51>

MEN'S ROOM SENRYU

golden scent of piss
everywhere porcelain gleams
macho graffiti

magic marker words
KEEP YOUR FAG EYES TO YOURSELF
this must be the place

tin booth called a stall
with a hole drilled through the wall
jagged edge   think twice

under the zipper
under the rugged façade
smoldering in vain

smell of loneliness
mixed with disinfectant smell
nobody is clean

no admission here
no means of future contact
all's anonymous

softer felt tip words
prophet in the wilderness
SILENCE EQUALS DEATH

zip up   head home   dream
names exchanged, and tenderness
hug pillow in sleep

<52>

THE HUSTLER

After Alexandra Grilikhes's poem, "The Statue"

A street hustler leans
on a grated storefront,
letting the lights
of cars passing
illumine his torso.

T-shirt
tight with one rip
under one armpit, cotton white
against tan flesh, stretching
when he half turns
to follow eyes
that take note of him.

Drivers in a slow line
circle the block like sharks.
Headlights make his shadow large.
His mind is
     hidden.
How much
will the money pay for,
how much more
if the spirit should move him?
Does he consider this
war, and would the cost
of a perceived loss set him off?

<53>

What is a man
to this fast-aging boy?
What's his measure
in a mirror?
Waves of heat
distort his face.
His signal
            wavers,
crackling
like a sudden fire.

ROUGH TRADE

To lean against a wall
and look that good
requires no practice,
just a knack
(and a strong back).

<54>

THE SON OF MAN

Last night on State Street
I saw Jesus — or at least
a good facsimile — hustling.
He had it all:
the hair, the beard,
the piercing eyes,
the hot glare of a man
with hidden wounds.
But his righteous anger
sabotaged his efforts;
no one slowed their car
to wave him over;
no one loitered at the corner,
looking back.

This was not the gentle Jesus
of the sixties,
borne aloft by soft black voices.
This was a Jesus
turned out on the street
by Republican congressmen
who call their cruelty "reform."
This was a new orphan Jesus —
disowned, or just abandoned,
by his father. This, too, was Jesus
on a burning cross, but no
Beatitudes would guide him.
This Jesus
did not have a dream.

<55>

I tried to scan him
but not catch his eye;
I was compelled,
but not at all attracted.
His hands, shoved in the pockets
of his grimy low-slung jeans,
could not be checked
for glowing wounds.
His sandaled feet
looked like they would pollute
most any water
they might walk on.
His chest was bare;
his side was bruised,
but whole.
He was fascinating
as a three-car crash
jamming the world's most mundane freeway.
He was the dark spot
in this sea of detail,
leaning on a brownstone wall.

When he caught me,
I was quick
to look way,
to walk away,
to get away;
he followed,
but just for a block.

<56>

I prayed my thanks
under my rapid breath;
his childhood and mine
would collide
like the nail and the wood.

All I could do
was save
myself.

<57>

BATHS POEM

Corridors of closed and open doors
we wander down like guests
on some surreal game show —
you pick out a stranger
as valve for your pressure,
as if your loneliness
were only steam.
Lights in the ceiling
make everyone's skin
look yellow as sliced lemons
propped on the lip of the mixed drink
you sipped hours ago.

Unlike the sweat on glass,
you can smell the sweat here —
that, and the acrid testosterone
haunting the halls. The towel
tucked into itself
around your waist
waits, impatient
to fall.

Eyes say "no"
as bitterly
as words, so some
seek group-grope rooms
where you can't see them,

<58>

rooms drenched
in darkness
or steam.

Out in the light,
there are some faces
that your eyes
might recognize:

The owner of your favorite restaurant
lies on his belly, and looks away quick
as you pass. The priest
who made your heart throb
back in high school
sees you in the locker room
and flees,
leaps into clothes
to hide his blush
from head to toe.
You want to tell him
to relax —
after all,
he's seen you, too,
and anyway, the year's
1974. We're supposed to be
beyond embarrassment.

<59>

But you're the one
who's here
looking for love, the one
these many instantaneous rejections
will leave marks on
for the longest. And
even invisible scars
show to the eyes
that prowl this place.

These cats shy away
from prey that looks deep
in their eyes.

<60>

A MAN MARRIES HIS TAN

Most of us want
a real man
for a husband —
someone loving, constant,
who will keep us warm.

This man
makes his marriage bed alone,
under a lid
whose artificial light
seems even brighter than the sun.
He's found his warmth
without the stress of company.
He wants to coat himself
with a disguising sheen
to wear even when naked.
It makes him look
healthy, outdoorsy,
though he's always tense
and spends his days
behind an office door.
This is more like the marriages
a lot of so-called "straight" men have —
one for the sake of appearances,
even his own appearance
in the mirror,
one that creates a vivid myth
of vibrant health
even he can believe.
after all, as they say,
seeing is believing.

<61>

In the old days,
there was one strip of fish white
at his middle when naked,
to remind him
that this marriage was a lie —
what an ironic wedding ring!
Now there's no need
even for that.
He can strip without fear
in the light,
yet not expose
the darkness of his life.
He can behave as though
he walks in endless summer,
in which sun shines
just for him,
even when everybody else he sees
is sneezing.
He can be the Adonis
of the indoor heated pool,
the one bronze god
to grace the pale-faced locker room.

Never mind how much
cold air may shrink his penis;
it will still be golden brown,
like a good sausage.
Not that he'd let anybody
put it in his mouth. No,
his new true color
is the only safe companion
for the most private of pastimes.

<62>

It's not disappointed
if his hair is not in place,
if he forgot deodorant,
or, worse, if he wakes up
in a foul humor.
It's as much a companion
as those super-lifelike dolls
he can't afford, which even
warm to the touch —
and which can't be deflated,
unlike his ego, so fragile,
so bitterly brittle.
And it won't try
to compete with him
or make him face
Any complaints.

He won't even have
to ask it
to take vows.
He knows it will never
betray or desert him,
so long as the salon stays open
and he can afford it —
that's the only way
this object of his love would fade.

Still, he is afraid
to do one thing
he feels a strong impulse to do.
He won't give it
a name.

<63>

It would have come to him with one
if it were human.
You *can* name
some things you purchase,
but he hesitates
to treat it like a dog.

ADVERTISING FOR LOVE

The model's projecting himself
through the camera lens — he's
the photographer, too —
like Narcissus, but he can't
fall through. He smiles
with blinding perfect teeth,
bats long-lashed eyes
clear as a lake
no-one's allowed
to swim in.
But I'd bet some
have drowned there.

<64>

A BILLION YEARS AGO

The bar called
The Brass Rail,
Asbury Park,
dead of winter,
the sand white,
his vehicle
parked right outside.
He had a Volkswagen
van, curtains
over the windows,
heater blasting,
a draft, icy,
whistling through.
We fucked our brains out
in the back
for hours. Took short breaks
to duck inside,
chug beers. Everybody knew
what we were up to,
watched us
make out at the bar.
The scandal
made it even more
exciting. He was bald
and lean, his chin
covered with stubble,
with a small welt
where I bit him.
I can't recall his name.
I don't know why
we didn't stay in touch.

<65>

It was like
fire in a bottle. Gulp it down
until it's gone,
and never think
that there won't be more
where it came from.
I thought I knew
what love was.

<66>

MY FIRST BISEXUAL

The man had a dent in his forehead, due
to childhood
spinal meningitis. But I fell
for the strange fellow
anyway. Maybe because
his beard
and one gold earring
made him look
piratical.

A potter he was,
and obsessed
about having
a son;
his constant talk about his need
to have a child —
which he described
as "biological" —
made him sound as though he
had something to prove.

His last name
was Hart, missing the e
for ease. It was difficult
for him to love.
The dust of his craft
was all over him;
his hands seemed determined
to shape everything.

<67>

After being locked inside
his box of fire,
my eyes glazed over
and I shattered. I suppose
he saw me
as a failed experiment.

My rival
made a better vessel
for his passion,
with her long black hair
so straight,
and her egg shape.
He told me that his orgasm
was never good with her —
she'd always have to use her hand
to finish him.
I guess she had
to reach inside herself
for seeding.
Her first name
came from the Old Testament,
so God
was on her side —
or was He? What was that old saying
about tears
and answered prayers?

<68>

I saw him
and his son together
years from then,
from a safe distance —
a little blonde copy
of him, soft
and ripe
for the shaping.

<69>

ALOFT

for Boruk

That 14th Street loft window's
always open, even on
the rainy days;

when skies
become street-colored, when carwheels
stream streets full of
running whispers.

I am thinking of
who watches through it,
whose beard, barely wet,
shines in the greyness;

I am thinking
about drinking in
his presence, in
midair, with all umbrellas
underneath me. I am thinking
of a street above the ground.

I'm
at window-level, head
thrown back, rain
running down my throat…

I am looking
to be seen
through, to stay
open.

<70>

THIS POEM SUCKS

Two shaved pink globes
nestle against
a bed of beard —
lips press
to the root of the riddle
of what makes you moan.
The tongue's tip slithers
slowly to the tower's peak,
to dance around the royal crown —
purple, not gold,
with its jewels now
much farther below
than they were
just moments ago.

Lava begins to bubble
in the back
of the equation
in your mind —
and suddenly another inch
insinuates itself
into the ever-longer
question.

The answer approaches —
its prophets,
a trickle of salt
and a twitch of the hips,
and a whimper
between your hoarse orders
so urgently whispered.

<71>

Sweat glistens
on your abdomen.
the smell and taste of you
intensify.

Come on baby, I say,
without a word
to interrupt
my lips and tongue.
Come on, I say,
*Come on and prove
the Big Bang Theory* —
a deep truth,
so hard to swallow.

<72>

RULE OF THUMB

As we kayak,
an alligator's eyes and nose
glide by us, and then
disappear straight down.

"He's a big one," you say.

"How big?"

"From the eyes to the nose,
figure a foot
for every inch."

I imagine your balls
on his skull
above his eyes,
and the tip
of your hard dick
between his nostrils —
a perfect fit.

But all I say is,
"Holy Shit!
He *is* a big one!"

<73>

THE MOMENT CAPTURES US

You lost control
of the kayak,
trying to turn it around.

I wanted a snapshot
of the alligator,
lounging on a log
stuck in the center
of the river.

The current
was stronger
than you were,
which shouldn't
have been
a surprise.

The 8-foot gator
turned his head,
eyes on the camera,
then dived
across my lap
into the water,
as the boat
and log
connected. Had he lashed
his tail, he might well
have broken my neck,
the way I know
you wanted to.

<74>

Meanwhile, my camera
was too cheap
to catch the moment;

all I have left
is a blur.

<75>

HOW...

How, at the beach,
he went much further out
than me,
riding big waves back in
while I just waded,
trying hard to keep my balance;

How he rowed behind me
in the boat,
controlled our motion;
how he took my oar
away from me,
saying my rowing
hampered more than helped;

How, later, I admired
his lighthouse painting
on black paper;
how he took it down
from the wall,
out of its frame,
rolled it up
and gave it to me —
much more freely
than that other gift
I craved, the gift
he would deny he gave;

<76>

How I missed my train home
by two short minutes
and sat stranded, alone,
for three hours
at the station,
waiting in the shadow
of the angel
lifting up the broken man, the great angel
of metal or stone —
black and shiny and certainly
hard, though I have never touched it —
the angel that my camera
would not capture,
suddenly run out of film —
a flash, yes, but nothing
to keep —

Even that *statue* of an angel,
even a statue,
just would not
stand still for me,
would not allow itself
to be caught
and brought
home.

<77>

IN PASSING

A pang of would-be pleasure
when you see his shoulder glisten
just that way, the way
it never will
again; you know
whatever happens
is once in a lifetime —
you've burned long enough
to learn. You will never
see again,
at just this angle,
this thing
no camera captures
like your eyes.

if you could,
you might ask him
to hold that pose,
to make believe
life is an art class,
let your look
last that much longer.
But a wave
knocks him off-balance,

And you turn
your glance away,
down to the dark edge
of white sand
that recedes
with the tide.

<78>

RETROACTIVELY ATTRACTIVE

When I am dead,
like many poets I admire,
people will wish I were alive.
Strangers will read my words
and grieve for me.
People I've lusted after from afar
will wish they'd balled me
while they had the chance —
maybe not revising their reaction,
but, at least,
just for the story.
They'll think of me
the way I think
of Allen Ginsberg.

<79>

WHEN I REINCARNATE

Forget this New Age princess
Shirley MacClaine stuff.

I want to come back as a biker chick,
get passed around (at first) from guy to guy
like a cheap bottle
that tastes better
than it should. Let me
get gang banged
on the green felt of
the pool table,
and leave a deep impression
of my legendary ass. Let me
rock the clubhouse
so they'll all want
one more taste,
although they never
dreamed they would. Let me
provide the inspiration
for knife fights
between the Bros,
for tattoos
that immortalize me —
till that fatal accident
or liver failure.

I want to be the subject of
a jukebox song, one
guys will wait in line to play.
Let me be
that mistake

<80>

that breaks up
the bland marriages
at last, and
let me be long gone
when hubby turns around.
Let me leave behind
the mark, the sting, the scent
that sticks
forever. Let me be like
the road
that left them
restless.

<81>

THREE WORDS LATER

I was just moving
from one spot to another;
it was nearly time
for our weekly event to start.
You were hanging by the doorway,
kidding
with another friend,
who gives you criticism,
about how gentle she is:
"You don't love me enough
to say nasty things to me,
like Jack;" I was meant to hear it,
and to laugh,
and I did —
but when I chimed in
to enjoy the laugh,
I got more
than I bargained for.

As the world segued into slow motion —
like in a movie sequence, music
heightening to show
significance —
I gently slid,
while passing by,
my right hand down your shoulders
to your back and said
"*I* love you;"
and over-emphasized the "I,"
for irony;

<82>

And then I felt
a wave I couldn't see
slam into me, as if we were wading waist-deep
at the edge of the sea
instead of schmoozing in the rainy city,
(and maybe we were,
in a way —
at any rate, I wasn't
where I'd thought I was.)
Although the wave washed through me,
more like energy than water,
there *was* roaring
in my ears for just that moment,
and I caught myself off-balance.

You laughed. The emcee called
for our attention.
We left our friend
and walked back to our table,
up near the front of the room.
We walked together
in a way we never had
before. Your face
was shining, suddenly lit up
by something.

I kept flashing back on
the electrical charge when I touched you
at the moment that I said I loved you
for another's benefit; rubbing your back,
saying it kiddingly
to magnify your point, and

<83>

it was like my touching you fulfilled a circuit
that was started in the saying;
sometimes when you say a thing
you realize it's true
for the first time —

I love you —

but I had no idea
what the repercussions of that fact,
(if there were any)
might be for us, or even
just for me.

For a moment after,
both of us were giddy;
I don't know if you knew why
or even noticed,
and I wanted to touch you again
in any way I could
that wouldn't seem invasive,
and when you sat beside me,
for a moment,
we shared
one warm pocket of space.

I didn't want
to pass beyond that moment,
to go back to how it was.
I wanted to wrap it around me,
to feel how it fit.

<84>

But I needn't have worried;
Now, when I look at you,
I see you in a new way —
my beholder's eyes
still catch that glow,
although my mind
is groping blind.

I only know
I told you that
I love you —

And I can't be sorry that I said it;
and I also know I meant it,
though I don't know yet
exactly what it means.

<85>

DISTANCES

We had spent the weekend
in Atlantic City,
back when there was a boardwalk
that had fortune tellers
and amusement piers —
before going there was a gamble.
We were both nineteen
and friends,
and nothing more.

Sunday evening,
on his way to drop me off,
he got
a costly parking ticket.
He didn't earn much
at his job in the shop
where so many poor poets
found they could afford
to sometimes make their photocopies.
He was upset;
we sat idling
in his grungy white VW
outside my house,
and it was time
to say goodbye.
Not thinking about it,
I hugged him, hoping
it would comfort him,
and nothing more.

<89>

I felt him freeze
in my embrace.
He pulled back,
looked at me
with horror. Neither of us
said a thing.
I got out of the car, and
he stomped on the gas
and screeched away, peeling rubber
in a cloud of smoke.
I just stood there in shock,
shaking my head.
We'd just spent two nights
alone in a hotel room,
and I'd never made a move.
And yet he was afraid
of my "intentions."

After that, we never spoke again.

The last time I saw him,
not long after that,
was one day at the printer's
where he worked.

I'd stopped by there
to see another friend.
He gave me an accusing look,
then fled to the back room
without a word, and stayed there
till after I'd left.

<90>

We had been friends,
or so I'd thought,
for several months.
He'd known I was gay;
I'd known he wasn't.
I'd had no problem with
our different preferences;
he'd shown no indication
he did, either.

I suppose I could have tried
to get in touch, to talk to him,
but I had nothing to explain —
and was, frankly,
too pissed off to try.
It was only a hug,
for Christ's sake.

So many friendships fall away
before the years go by —
before you learn to read
all of the subtle signs,
the wordless signals
people send,
the rules
that aren't spoken.

Andy, I forget
your last name now —
but even
if I knew how, I still
wouldn't contact you.

<91>

It was all
too long ago,
at this point.

Yet I still feel
that moment when you froze,
still see that bald look
of betrayal,
that's my only souvenir
of our trip "down The Shore."

And there is no more
naïve Atlantic City,
only someplace cold
and overpriced
to play games where
only money
is at risk,
where grown-ups go to take
their kind of chances.

<92>

AT HOME

Nice weather today.
We're standing
on our doorstep,
chatting.

Two teenage boys
walk by
in the middle
of the street.
They're both
staring at us
intently.
I meet their eyes
as if to say,
"What is the problem?
Is it my hump,
or the horns?"

One nudges the other
and says, just loud enough
so we can hear,
"I told you —
They're faggots.
See how
they're staring at us?"

<93>

The man who lives next door to us
has stopped saying hello.
At first, we thought he was
preoccupied; he's always working
on something —
washing the car, filling his fountain
with fish, trimming the lawn.

Then, the other day,
we happened to run into him
inside the tiny pizza shop
that's halfway down the block.
There, in a space so small
there's hardly room to turn around,
he wouldn't even look at us.
And we were close enough
to see his look of fear.
It seemed to make things worse
that we were on a first name basis
with the workers,
and that they all kidded with us.
I tried to catch his eye,
and swear I saw him break a sweat.
I asked you, "Isn't that our neighbor?"
to make sure he didn't have a crazy twin.

When he finished his business,
he didn't just leave — he fled.
We couldn't help but laugh —
it was so strange. His wife
and three kids always say hello;

<94>

so do his parents, who lived
in their house before they did.
And so did he, at first.

Until he thought, I guess,
about what it implies
when two middle-aged guys
can live together
right next door. Maybe it blurs
his vision of the world,
apparently not shared
with even his own family.

But I wasn't about to pat his back
and say, "Poor baby,
don't be scared; we're harmless."
I felt sure he would misunderstand the gesture.

<95>

He shows up beside you
at the bar.
You've stopped in
to recuperate from work
before the shaky subway sojourn
home. You imagine
he has, too.

You've never liked him
all that much. Easier
to keep him friendly, though.
You tell him you're doing OK
and let him ramble.

He goes on about Elaine.
Her cubicle
is not that far from yours
or his. He tells you
she's a lesbian.
He heard her
talking to her girlfriend
on the phone, then
glimpsed them
meeting on the street.
You barely know the girl,
but like her more
than him — seems like
a reasonable person.

<96>

You nod
and grunt, expressing
no opinion.
He reads this
as a show of interest,
keeps on talking,
gathering excitement, wonders
if you've pictured girls together.
It's clear to you
that he has.
You say nothing, stare
into the depths of your beer.

He says he bets
that a real man
could change Elaine.
She wouldn't want a woman
if she tried
a guy like you,
for instance.
You check his eyes
and see
he's also pictured
that. And he wants
to plant that picture
in your head, hopes
you'll tell him
if anything happens.

You down
your nearly full beer
in one gulp,
slap the tip
on the bar, check

<97>

your watch. You lose track
of the rest of what
he's saying. Your partner
is waiting at home. This guy
has no clue who you are.

Outside,
you walk briskly alone.
the smog-infested air seems
fresh and sweet.
Even the screeching subway
sounds like music.

<98>

"You're gay,"
said Craig, as if
that made me an expert
on how we all are.
"Do you like
young kids?"

"Like" was the loaded word,
despite the lack of emphasis.

I decided not to be
defensive.
"I just don't think of people that age
in that way," I said, and
truthfully. (My type has always been
older than me).

Maybe I should have told him
that men molest girls
far more often than boys,
that most child rape
occurs within the family,
a favorite crime
of trusted uncles.

He was the sort
who would enjoy statistics,
though his T-shirt
showed a picture
of the Bible,
with the slogan

<99>

LIFE:
READ THE INSTRUCTIONS.

But we had
a gig
to get on with —
he had to do sound;
I had to sing.
We both had parts to play,
as destiny dictated.

<100>

THE SLAM GOES UP IN SMOKE

God, I'd like to take
a big drag on a cigarette —
it's been so long.

Remembering the night
I stormed out of
the slam, sat at
the bar and filled my lungs
with burning menthol
I'd just bought
from a machine.

And the black dude
who had read the homophobic poem
and got the huge reaction
that drove me out of the room
came up and stood next to me
with no idea who I was,
to get a drink,
and I just answered his hello
like it was nothing,
thinking maybe I should even
offer him a blowjob
just to blow his mind.
And Randy, the slam organizer,
sidled up to me
and said, "I didn't think you smoked,"
and I spat out, "I don't,"
and left, and never came again,

<101>

boycotting
the damn slam
forever.

Smoke,
and the memory of smoke,
have teeth for me.
The word
"slam"
has more than one meaning.

Later, I'd explain
the how and why
of my perpetual new absence.
But for now,
I'd suck the fumes
that killed my father
and march out into the night,
a private kind
of Pride Parade.

Only the taste of smoke
is a fond memory,
a measure of defiance,
doing something
that is not
"normal"
for me.

<102>

TO A GOOD CHRISTIAN
AT THE WEEKLY OPEN READING

You don't meet anyone's eyes
when you arrive.
Sometimes we say hello
when we first see you —
then we talk around you
like you aren't there.
But we do know your name.
You don't appear to know
any of ours.

This week,
you're wearing headphones.
You will wear them
until you get up to read.
I hope that
makes this easier for you.

When it's your turn
at the podium —
before you read
your latest
fire and brimstone rant —
you say that some of us
have got the wrong idea.
Christians, we believe,
think that they're better than us.

<103>

That isn't the case —
or shouldn't be. Christians
shouldn't act
as though they are,
since that creates
stereotypes.

You know only too well
that you're no better than us.
You lust after women,
for example. And you did lots of
bad, bad things
before you were saved.
You know you are
also
a sinner.

Then, one of us asks you a question:
"Do you think you're the only Christian here?"
You look all around the room, admitting,
"I don't know,"
as if you've never really
looked at us before,
though you've been coming here for months.
There is a long moment of silence.

But, of course,
nobody volunteers
their truth to you.

<104>

I wonder, once again,
just what you want from us.
I don't think
I need to wonder
what you have assumed about us,
though I, too,
have made assumptions
about you.

One
is that you project
the category "sinner"
onto all the rest of us.
And that's the domino
that sets all others
falling.

<105>

PASTOR DAMON

The fundamentalist evangelist
looks like a convict —
beard, long hair, one arm
sleeved with tattoos —
but he wants to be the warden
of this naïve congregation.
His ministry
is aimed at teens, a population
easy to delude.
So he plays hardball
with their fear of
their own hormones,
their own wakening desires.
He calls the ones
"tormented by the demon
homosexuality"
to make their way
down to the front at
the foot of the stage,
where they weep and prostrate themselves.
He tells them they can
"pray the gay away."
One girl confesses, weeping,
through a handheld microphone,
that she has been
called names, ridiculed,
and persecuted
by her "normal" classmates.
Why can't she see
that here's more of the same?

<106>

She volunteers herself
for more abuse,
of a more sinister variety;
abuse that masquerades
as sympathy. Pastor Damon smiles,
and puts one ink-stained arm
around her. Her life so far
has been so circumscribed
that she can't see her "helper"
as he is —
a dangerous piece of rough trade,
trying to coerce corroboration
of the lies he tells himself,
about himself. Self-hatred is
the product this man's hawking.
He swoops down on her
as if she were a mouse.
She only sees
the shadows of the wings
he wears, and not
his predatory purpose, nor
the slashing beak
he hides behind his Jesus beard.
She hasn't noticed how his first name,
Damon, is one letter off
from "Demon."

<107>

ON FEELING SURROUNDED

If I kissed my lover
on the subway, many people
would go mad.

Some of them are wives
or husbands; few of them
are lovers

when the word means "Lover"
as I understand it.

They would make me
a defendant, find me guilty
of their madness
and my kiss.

Through much of history
I haven't kissed my lover,
even when there were no subways.

Through many incarnations
I was guilty,
but I won't be guilty
now…

And so,
I kiss my lover, and
he

<108>

flinches, feeling
watched;
but flinches
grinning, knowing

this
is the beginning.

<109>

I stand before my enemies,
anointed in eye shadow.
I never did like purple,
but I chose it
because it is the color of confession.
I confess I am what these hunters
would aim for
with their blunt arrows of fear,
seeking to kill
the hidden qualities
I mirror, when I paint myself
for love, and not
for war.

The rabbit's eyes are on the side
to warn him
of what's creeping up on him,
to give him lots of time
to flee. I am
as gentle
and as fragile,
but I look straight on
at what comes after me.
There will always come a momentary
meeting of the eyes,
so I can haunt these predators
after they chase me,
wound me,
even if they kill me,

<110>

I am the wild spirit
shot down like a fallen star
into their midst,
in this country
they think they have tamed.

<111>

WATER

Strike no starting pose —
just jump in
as you are.

So you can't
dive
into a pool; you
don't know how;
you never learned
when you were young enough;
now, your aging back
just couldn't take the strain, but
you still want
to swim.

The water
lets you in,
opens itself,
enfolds, supports
you, takes its cue
from you,
breaks up
in splashes
when you
thrash your limbs,
shapes itself
around you
when you wade,

<112>

closes
behind you
when you sink
and disappear
deliberately.

Once, at the Jersey shore,
that crucible
of childhood changes,
you went wading
chest-deep
through the waves,
letting them
lift you and
carry you backwards.
You were
minding your own business,
having fun. A nearby
blonde boy
called you
"Faggot."
You asked,
"What?" He said,
"You heard me."

You had, but
you didn't get
why. The water
held you, just the same
as it held him.
The sea clearly
had room
for both
of you.

<113>

Pools and lakes
are even
more accepting
than the ocean,
not resisting you
at all, like
some long-time love
who freely chooses
you.

Let the water
wash what
weight we bear
away. It's wide
and deep enough
to hold us all.

<114>

CONDITIONS

GULLS

Lately, gulls invade
the parking lots
of restaurants we often visit.
When I was young, I only saw them
at the seashore. I can't guess
what's driven them inland —
far from waves, wet sand,
and shellfish washing up
for them to eat. Maybe they like
greasy diner food.

I always found the sound of them
unsettling — those cries
that seem so lonely
even when there's
a whole flock; what
are they mourning? My grandmother
said they were dead souls
afraid to be angels. But her husband
hated them. They'd swarm his boat,
hungry for bait. He swore
they scared off the fish.

Once, he yelled obscenities at me
for feeding them. I had to stop.
Then one swooped down
and snatched his hat
right off his head,
and dropped it in the sea.
Maybe that's why I've admired them
ever since.

<117>

They are white, like the souls
St. Joseph's nuns scratched
on their blackboards with loud chalk.
I still wish I could see them
gliding over white-capped water.

But, my limits
being what they are, I'll settle
for a parking lot —
a fittingly earthbound setting
in which to be reminded
of my old, and never quenched,
longing to fly.

<118>

When I worked at Morrow's Nut House
during high school,
a pigeon flew in through the front door,
held open too long
by an elderly lady
while she lugged in one bag too many.
Grey-headed, red-footed
and gurgling, the bird dodged my broom
and fluttered under the display case glass,
flopping down on a sticky arrangement
of bright green jellied candies,
huddling there as if to hide
in the midst of its own ruffled feathers.
It cooed and clucked
and poked its head around,
and looked up curiously,
and didn't peck me
when I picked it up,
took it outside on Market Street,
and gave it back to a warm breeze
laced with exhaust fumes.

My next task, dictated
by my sour-faced old maid boss,
with pale hands withered like dried fruit,
was to pick out what fragments of
feather and other debris
the "damn bird" might have left behind,
and put the candy
back out there for sale.
I did as I was told,

<119>

remembering his heartbeat in my hands,
and how my mother always said
pigeons were filthy,
full of lice and strange diseases.
He hadn't seemed itchy or sick,
just a little perplexed —
and when he'd flown away,
I envied him.

I didn't last at Morrow's Nut House.
I got fired for calling off
due to a favorite uncle's
unforeseen demise,
and never held a pigeon
in my hands again.

Now I only stop in Philadelphia
to change trains on my way
to New York City,
which I only visit rarely.
In 30th Street Station,
there's a food court;
if there's time, I find a table
and I write.
There's always a pigeon or two
that gets into the station,
and wanders on the floor
between the tables,
bobs its head hunting for scraps,
cooing and burbling.

<120>

One table I picked
was spattered with white droppings.

People ignore the pigeons
or they feed them,
killing time till the next train.
I watch and wonder
at their lack of fear,
clutching a ticket
I'd never need
if I had wings.

<121>

GULLS, PIGEONS,
AND HARE KRISHNAS

Gulls perched on the wall
watch humanity pass
with no apparent interest.
When you can fly,
what else
grabs your attention?

A Hare Krishna told me once
whatever fills your mind
most often
determines how
you'll be reborn.
If you fixate
on sex, you'll come back
as a pigeon. "A dirty
bird," he said, sounding
like a grouchy grandpa.

I pointed out to him
that pigeons can fly.

Flying seems
exhilarating
when you can't do more
than dream about it.
And I dream about it
often. Always have.

<122>

Hare Krishnas,
on the other hand,
I only see in dreams
if it's a nightmare.
Those who cannot fly
hang out in airports,
knowing what they do
in spirit
can't come true
until they die,
and airports
are a sort of
consolation prize.
There, Krishnas fixate on
the folks with lots of
baggage, who can't
get away as quickly;
them, they'll stop
and badger
with their version
of the truth.

Gulls and pigeons
bring
only a song —
gurgles of warmth,
cries of
release,
the language
of the winged

<123>

who know
only this moment,
who can fly
without waiting in line
to buy a ticket,
whose truth
waits for them
somewhere
high in blue air.

<124>

The man has a stone
in his pocket;
smooth and black,
it has the power
to absorb a person's
pain.

He never uses it, though,
just keeps it with him —
in case. It's small,
flat, light,
fits easily
with keys
to houses he no longer
visits, and the coins
he will not spend.
His pocket crowds
with possibilities.

He walks with his head down,
always afraid
he might fall — or worse,
someone
might see
the look
in his eyes.
He hoards his secrets,
and he hides his love.

<125>

After the winter,
he tells himself,
he will peel off
his dead skin,
and allow the sun in.
Till then, the season may
surround,
but cannot touch him.

<126>

Freezing February night. Switching trains.
Manhattan subway stop — wish I could remember
the street number. Near a college, the sign said
(can't remember which one).
Been about 25 years,
but I'll never forget
what I saw there:

Long, narrow platform; no one on it
on foot
but me and a beat cop in uniform.
Station deserted except for him, me
and a couple of homeless guys
passed out on two of the benches.
I didn't care, being
too nervous to sit
anyway.

Anyway, this cop strolls up to one,
twirling his nightstick
as if it were a baton. Suddenly
he grips it by the handle,
hauls off
and slaps it hard
against the soles of the guy's feet.
I thank God he's wearing shoes.
The loud crack makes me jump,
although I saw it coming.

<127>

The guy barely revives, looking up
puzzled, luckily
anesthetized on something
strong.

The cop says, voice ringing out
off of the concrete, "Those benches
are for PEOPLE,
not you guys." Then he looks back,
flashes me a smile, white
as a blackboard soul drawn by a nun
under his little Hitler moustache.
He expects to see
approval
in my face.
I feel sick, look
down. I can't
meet his eyes.
I can't let him see
my revulsion
or, even worse,
my fear that
he'll focus
his agitation
on me. *Please,*
just let me be,
I think. *Don't*
make me part of your
mad trip to nowhere.
I'm just in the wrong
place, wrong time.
I worked late.
I'm just trying to get
home.

<128>

THE SLOW MURDER
OF TAYLOR MEAD

Taylor Mead, Dec. 31, 1929 - May 8, 2013

Taylor Mead, a fixture in the Lower East Side as well as Andy Warhol's
Factory scene back in the day, died yesterday while in Colorado. The
legendary Lower East Side artist, poet and actor died after suffering a
stroke. The 88-year-old was temporarily living in Colorado after vacating
his longtime Ludlow Street apartment in April. The rent-stabilized space,
which he lived in for 34 years, was costing him just $380 a month. He
"was battling with a developer who is converting the rest of the
building's apartments into market rate apartments."

—5/9/2013 obituary in The Gothamist

Andy Warhol made a film about your ass —
an hour of just your butt. He even called it
Taylor Mead's Ass. I never saw it —
the film, that is. Well, I never
saw your ass, either.
I only met you
after you were old,
a beloved Lower East Side character
brimming with stories,
keeping alive and vivid
certain moments in our history
when it seemed like all doors
had been thrown open.
You could hold court
like the best of queens —
although you lived in squalor
as a pauper, you had royal memories.
You swept away realities
that might make squeamish

<129>

your delighted listeners,
and let us all laugh at a past
when things were sillier
and simpler, when a soup can
could be art.

But Taylor, now your celebrated ass
is nowhere to be found.
It's not like
the scarecrow in *The Wizard of Oz* saying,
"that's me all over,"
although you would have camped it up at least that much.
Perhaps it wasn't quite
as literal, but you were
torn apart, nevertheless —
and flesh and blood, unlike
a mess of straw, can't be
scooped up and
stuffed back in.
And the figurative
sometimes can
prove fatal.

You were 88 years old
when, at long last,
your sneering landlord
murdered you. You'd lived in
your fifth floor apartment for
34 years, just one year less
than your landlord had been alive.
You'd been one of the last tenants left,
hanging on to your rent-controlled flat,
in the building he had turned into
a dirty, dangerous construction site,

<130>

so people were forced
to evict themselves
or face extinction by their own environment.

And so you lived with
constant hammering
from dawn till night,
plaster in your hair
and eyes, roaches
crawling up your legs,
holes drilled through your wall,
a constant fog of dust.

A younger person would have
found all that nightmarish —
hard to imagine
how you lived with it for months.
Nearly 90, you were so feeble
that you could barely stand.
You'd only leave the place
a time or two each week —
the journey down from the faraway top floor
was quite a trek for you.

But your landlord, a millionaire brat
who had just entered middle age,
seethed in a chronic rage
that rent control prevented him
from charging more than
four hundred a month
for your absurdly crumbling hovel.
All around you, having driven
all your neighbors out,
he built more passable apartments,

<131>

planned to rent them out
for nearly eight thousand a month.
His company was, after all,
called Magnum Real Estate,
named for the notorious gun
that made Clint Eastwood's day.
The man identifies
with deadly weapons.
He kept on making matters
worse and worse.
The nightmare
he put you through
lasted
for nearly a year.

At last, gasping,
you gave up on breathing dust,
and you signed some sort of agreement,
and you went to stay with relatives
in Colorado, planning to "come home" soon
to New York. But less than a month later,
a stroke killed you. And let's face it —
one stroke was brought on by another,
a stroke of fate that where you lived
became the property
of a rich pig whose greed
just endlessly expands,
free of all conscience
or of external restraint.
You just joined a long list
of this rapacious monster's conquests:
along with the low-income nursing home
he razed, replaced with new luxury condos,
or the lady who required a rescue

<132>

after his crew had ripped out her staircase.
You were just another object in his path
to be torn out and tossed away.
Your spirit was so strong
that your reaction was delayed a little bit,
but there's no doubt where the blame lies;
just weeks ago, a friend predicted
this would kill you, and was quoted
in the press. "This is elder abuse," he said.
"It's pretty Third World when you think about it."
Predictably, the landlord didn't listen.
In fact, another paper quoted him
as saying he deserved "a pat on the back"
for all the renovations he was doing. I say,

curse the bastard forever. Let Fate "pat his back"
with a sledgehammer — better yet,
a wrecking ball.

<133>

ONE COLD NIGHT

An icy night;
The pavement
was a slippery sheet
of danger underneath
even the surest feet. I stepped gingerly
out of our small car
onto the drugstore
parking lot. It was dark;
the only light
shone over the back doors.
Carefully, I waddled
toward the light,
in steps too small,
for fear of falling.

A van was parked
three spaces down,
its motor running.
A small, frail old woman
got out of the passenger side,
wobbling, unsteady,
with a cane.
She looked as if she'd break
if she should fall.
She looked pained
and afraid.
She looked at me
and asked,
"Sir, can you help me?"

<134>

Though the ground kept threatening
at every step to slide out
from beneath my feet,
I said, "Of course,"
and I gave her my arm.
We toddled toward the store.

Suddenly her son —
well, I assumed he was —
burst from the van behind us, slammed its door
behind him, hulked into our path,
a big bear of a man.
He thrust his scowling face
so close to mine
that I could smell smoke in his beard.
"WHAT'S GOIN' ON HERE?" he demanded.

"She asked me to help her," I said.
He snatched her roughly away
by her thin arm —
I feared for a moment she'd fall —
and muttered angrily,
ignored her explanations,
as he yanked her toward the store.
Me, he never gave a second look,
and I was, frankly, glad of that.
But I wondered, if the guy
felt so protective,
why he'd let her
walk that far on ice alone,
and hadn't even helped her
leave the van.

<135>

Then I stepped, grateful,
down the frozen concrete stairs,
felt warmth and light
surge over me,
saw shelves of fragile
and expensive gifts —
ceramic frogs with fishing rods
and such.
For a moment,
I forgot
why I was there,
lost in the gleam
as it hit me.

Then I turned
toward the back counter
to refill my medication
for depression.

<136>

SISTER SNAP

A photo catches three nuns
walking past a wall
spray-painted with graffiti
in a foreign language
somewhere in America.

One nun looks back
at the photographer,
and thinks
Fuck you
in English.

Unlike the graffiti,
her look,
I can read.

<137>

RAIN DANCE

for Ron

You ran outside
to dance
under the cloudburst,
get yourself
drenched,
tempt the lightning.

You peeled up your T-shirt,
pulled out the waist
of your jogging pants,
both front and back,
to catch as much rain
as you could, then
struck a goofy ballet pose.
And you kept
looking back at us, grinning
to please
your dry-humored audience,
safe behind the store front window.

"You know, he does
no drugs or alcohol,"
your former girlfriend told me,
"He just gets like this
naturally."

<138>

I laughed, dismissed
the strike of
inner lightning
waking up the dancer
long asleep in me,
whose wounds no longer let him
run out in the rain.

<139>

BARE-HEADED

If the man who has Style is going bald, he doesn't buy a hairpiece;
he shaves his head. You go *with* the tide, only faster.
— Quentin Crisp, in *An Evening With Quentin Crisp*

The bald man
likes things clear
and clean.
His loss was also growth;
he beat the tide
to shore, razor
in hand.
he cut his losses.
They say that bald men
have more hair
on their bodies
than on their heads,
that being bald
betrays
a greater potency.
Even
the Buddha
chose baldness —
and this
from a man
who'd transcended
desire.

<140>

The bald man
is brave.
He will not
wear toupees.
He will not
hide his beacon
under hats.
He demands
you take him
as he is
before you even
know his name.

The bald man
waves to Death
across the desert,
as if welcoming him
gladly. After all,
how much of a threat
can the hooded Death be,
compared to a man
who shines
the naked truth?

<141>

PICK-UP

It'd be nice
to meet a nice guy,
she thought, wandering
down the hill to the dirt road
that passed her parents' property.
Or just to get stoned,
added the devil
on her shoulder.
She thought she was smart.
She thought she knew
the way the whole world worked,
although she hadn't seen
that much of it.
She thought she was tough —
defying her father,
wearing tube tops,
smoking cigarettes.

The pick-up
had no license plate,
but she could only see it
from the front.
The driver wore
a baseball cap,
like every other guy
around these parts.
His windows were rolled down,
but she could smell
the sweet-rot odor
of pot smoke.

<142>

He leaned over,
popped open the door
on the passenger side.
She caught his smirk at her
and glanced uphill
at her family's sagging house, feeling
a fleeting spooky twinge,
but never dreamed
that this would be
her last look at her home.

It would be about a week
before the local paper noted
that she'd vanished,
and dozens of men
in baseball caps
would fan out through the woods
in search of her —
half of whom
had picked her up
at that same spot,
though only one
had done more with her than just flirt.
All of them knew
the girl was jailbait.

<143>

FERAL CHILD

At first, they thought
it was a raccoon
rooting through their trash,
leaving a mess
on the back porch.

But one night, Lizzie
got a glimpse of him.
After she switched on the light,
he was gone in a second.
She never saw a person
move so fast.
Though it was fall
and cold, the boy
was naked, but
she barely saw his body.

For that instant, her eyes
got locked with his:
wide, green, wild, and full of —
was it fear? His face
was framed in crazy hair
that stuck out on all sides
and had leaves in it,
(and lice too, she would have bet).
Then he was a blur,
shooting off toward the trees.

<144>

She'd been half asleep,
And stumbled back to bed.
She'd sleep no more that night,
though there would be
no more disturbances to hear.
How old was he, she wondered.
It had left her, not afraid,
but more unsettled,
her old view of life disrupted
by this unpredicted possibility.

She woke up her Charlie.
He called the police.
They went out back
with flashlights, poked around.
One stepped in human dung
wiped on dry leaves.
The other said they'd had a similar report
about a week ago — a woman
down the block — and she'd
been able to describe him.
He didn't sound like any
missing children from this area.
Liz shuddered, picturing a tribe
of missing children
living hidden in the woods,
something like *Lord of the Flies*.

But she felt sure
That this boy wasn't missing;
he'd been lost since birth.
His parents were not
looking for him.

<145>

She felt sure
there were no words
for what he'd been through.
She wondered whether she
should leave food on the back porch,
keep the kid
from messing up their trash —
well, OK, keep the kid
from starving. She flashed briefly on him
catching birds for food,
dismissed the image quickly
lest it clarify too much
and nauseate her.

As far as they knew, he never
tried their house again. But from that night on,
she would keep the cat inside.

<146>

SIDESHOW

SUBTEXT

At the local K-Mart,
an announcement
interrupts the music service —
a mechanical male voice
that says,
"Service needed
in Men's Wear."

The music comes back on,
plays for one bar.
Then another announcement,
and this time the robot voice
is female —
"Help needed
in Cosmetics."

Once more the music resumes.
The customers
think that they're shopping,
as they dance
to tunes they don't
consciously hear.

Men
need service;
women
need help.

<149>

...LIKE A GREEK STATUE

He's just like anyone you'd meet in Greek mythology.
—Dianne Chambers in "Cheers"

All the Greek gods got frozen in stone
forever, as if they'd seen
Medusa. And they were all naked
at the time. And they all have
such tiny schlongs.

You'd think
turning a man hard forever
would incline to have
the opposite effect. I guess
it was cold in ancient Greece.

Photography, sadly, cannot improve
on sculpture. And even if you rub
stone, it only gets
warmer, not larger.

Some non-prescription pills
sold by our late-night infomercials
would have been a big hit
on Olympus.

<150>

MEDUSA

Long after the hissing
had driven me mad,
long after the venoms
had twisted their roots
in my brain,
he finally came:

naked
except for his shield, bearing
a sword — symbol
of liberation in religions
I would never live to see.

He would not
look at me, but
at my image
mirrored in his shield,
the shield
he clearly didn't bring
to hide behind;
he had nothing to hide.
His nakedness
was beautiful. His sword
would liberate me

from my body
and its thousand passions
I could never quench.

<151>

I felt them rage
for the last time
as I looked at him,
flooded
with grave fascination.

Even if he could come close,
the lightnings in my hair
would strike him down.
I lived beyond touch —
a high price
of my own
bitter nature.

So I looked at him,
and drank him in,
and let him stalk me,
longing for the slice
to cut me loose
from my unbearable
awareness,
from my sleepless
smoldering.
I met his eyes
in that mirror,
and gave my consent,
burnt out from centuries
of living in my head.

<152>

Of all men, he alone
would glimpse my face
reflected there
and live,
and notice
it was radiant with anguish,
and be haunted
by regret.

Better to be
turned to stone,
believe me.

<153>

LEDA CONCEIVES

In our modern era,
the majority religion
in some countries
has a myth
of a divinely sired
child god
born from a human woman's
womb. His insemination
was spiritual, mysterious —
a miracle;
announced first by an angel,
though his mother
never had a choice,
although she did give her consent.
She was handed a prediction
it would happen,
and instructed
about what to name the boy.
It was clear to her
one must obey
an angel of the Lord,
acting on orders
from his Boss.

But sometime earlier,
in ancient Greece,
where nobody pretended
to be anything
but pagan,
they had myth makers
who did things

<154>

differently. They saw no need
to say it wasn't
rape.

So Zeus did not appear so civilized.
He sent no angel
with polite announcements,
though the thing did come
with wings, but
there were no pretensions
of humanity.

Some women say
all men are beasts;
some gods are, too.
sometimes —
this one did not deny it.
He fixed it
so that she could not
consent, not even
had the thought
occurred to her.

It seemed
an attack from the wild,
a pure burst
of brute force,
and not from a human with whom
one could argue or beg.
It did not seem
to happen
by design
at all, divine
or otherwise;

<155>

No, she was taken
by instinct,
and, afterward,
her own
instinct
took over.

The animal in her
knew what to do.
When she woke up
beside an egg,
after a bloody sojourn
through unconsciousness for —
well —
God knows how long,

She didn't know
where in her body
it had come from,
since her shape
looked as before,
and since the pain
throbbed everywhere.

She only knew
she must protect it,
hide it,
keep it.
And she knew this
with a fierceness
she had never felt
in any other knowledge.

<156>

She would not
have long to wait.
She feared that what came out
might fly away —
and, she admitted to herself,
half hoped it, too.

But when the shell broke,
there were no wings to unfold,
although there was a flash
in which the fragments of the shell
evaporated, and its viscous fluids
with it. The small, silent
explosion
left no evidence
of anything
unusual.

She learned soon
that it was only the next day,
that the whole pregnancy
and hatching
had unraveled
in twelve hours, like
some wild wine-distorted
nightmare. She might
have told herself
that that was all it was,
were it not
for the hatched brood,
especially
the girl;

<157>

the girl
with luminous
and haunting
eyes,
the girl
that no man
could resist,

the girl
they would call Helen —
a name whose meaning
her own story
would infuse
forever
with a lethal beauty,
a girl whose streak of the
divine
would not require proof
like a halo,
or wings.

<158>

OLYMPIAN CHESS

A whale is swimming
in the wine glass
on the chessboard.
Zeus takes a sip,
puts the glass back.
The whale, startled,
thrashes its tail,
spurts a geyser of wine
from its blow hole.
Unlike Zeus, the whale
is getting drunk, drunker and drunker
with each breath it takes.

Elsewhere on the board,
the gladiator, angel, duck and frog
are plotting their escape in whispers.
Zeus, who knows everything,
finds this amusing
to no end. But he makes a mental note
not to give the pieces
consciousness next time. Across the board, Hera —
whose mind he cannot read,
since she's a woman *and* his equal —

cooks up her own plot,
and discusses it
with no one.

<159>

PREY PER VIEW

National Aquarium, Baltimore, MD
Shark Alley Exhibit

You descend into the Shark Alley exhibit,
walking slowly down a ramp
that takes you deeper; with
dark red carpet silent underfoot.

The three-story tank wraps around
the dimly lit space
that contains you; its outer glass
is your walls, too;
you have air
on your side — water
is on theirs. Inside the tank,
the sharks will circle you
continuously, since
there's nowhere else
for them to go. There's only room
to swim
in one direction.

As you descend, the sharks
come swimming toward you;
soon they pass behind you, then
turn back, just as you turn
down one more level of the ramp,
like the next flight
of a tall stairwell,
and you find the same sharks
facing you again.

<160>

At least, it seems
like the same sharks.
They're all big, and
all look somewhat alike.
You really aren't sure
how many sharks
there are.

The only sound's
the ventilation system,
and the low hum
of the tanks. You wish
there were some music, and
you tell that to your friend,
and he makes you
regret it right away — he grins
and starts to hum
the theme from *Jaws*.
You elbow him; he laughs
and stops.

All the while, the sharks
keep circling you,
the way they would
if you were in the water,
where their circling
would foreshadow
an attack. They'd be
checking you out then,
noting your size, your speed,
your smell, your seeming
weaknesses, reading
your tiniest pulsations.

<161>

In here, you don't even know
if they're aware of you.
You can see them —
why shouldn't they see you? —
but they don't seem to notice you.
They glide
as if the tank were
the whole world,
both earth and sky
to their black eyes.
They almost seem mechanical,
not quite
alive. But you,
your heart pounds
and your breath
comes fast. For once,
despite the greyness
of the day outside,
the dullness of the job
you'll focus on again
tomorrow, you're acutely
sure
that you don't want
to die.

<162>

SLASHER MOVIE

We see from his viewpoint,
through holes in a mask,
and yet we don't identify with him.
The point is not
that we see what he sees;
we see what his victims
don't see, and thus,
feel more afraid for them.

What, are they deaf, too?
Don't they hear the music
warn of his approach?
How easy life would be
if music warned you
when bad scenes were imminent.

The victim is a girl, of course,
oblivious and vulnerable,
ripened to be sacrificed
to lusts she has no clue
that she's inspired. No,
she isn't being punished;
it takes awareness
to commit a sin.
But the killer
is unaware, too —
his victim is not real to him —
and so we label him "crazy"
as if that explains him.

<163>

He has no motive
and no motivation;
He even has no face
throughout most of the movie.
He has only camera eyes —
they just record
for later fantasizing —
and he has the knife,
the only tool
with which he'll penetrate.
We assume
all this is sexual, of course.

For this man —
we assume it's a man —
to kill is just a habit,
a mechanical compulsion,
fueled by impulse
that arises, automatic,
when it's triggered
by the proper stimulus.

The girl must be half-naked
and young,
and must try to survive
once the pain wakes her up.
Her motivation,
we all understand.

<164>

She's the one
who just wants to keep
breathing.
We identify with her,
and, for a little while,
we aren't bored to death.

<165>

I WANT A LOVER WITH A NAKED FACE

The mask is wood,
inflexible — not meant
to move with the face.
Its expression
is fixed, carved in
and painted on.
Anger moved the hands
that made the mask,
and under the anger hid fear,
like a long-buried face.

The mask is lacquered, red
with yellow streaks
smeared on its cheeks;
its eyebrows, strips
of pelt left over
from some luckless animal.
Put it on, and see the world
through holes, as if the world
were what is missing.
Perhaps the maker
meant to hang it
on a door
and not a face —
as a warning,
and not a disguise.

<166>

The killer in these movies
wears a mask, always;
to hide, not his identity,
but ugliness from his
deforming childhood,
or from the trauma of a fire;
when you finally see his true face,
it's too late, as if
the mask alone
were not reason to run.

Perhaps the mask
protects the killer
from the mirror
he's not brave enough
to face. At least
it gives his victims
more fair warning
than a mask
made out of words —
or the sighs
and caresses that say,
"It won't happen again."

They make leather masks
for consenting adults,
with zippers
to seal off the eyes
and mouth,
should you need
someone else
to oppress you
for fun.

<167>

Children don their masks
at Halloween,
when unreal faces
seem most festive;
it's such a giddy game
then, while they still
think it's all play.
In societies like ours,
we start them young.

THE SPIDERMAN POEMS

He doesn't have 8 legs,
but he does have 8 inches;
funny, one sees
no evidence of this
through his tight costume.

     ***

Tarzan did it first —
swinging
from one big phallic object
to another.
Of course, Tarzan's
points of reference
were not designed
by architects
who had to compensate.

     ***

Sometimes
he's more brutal
to villains

if he gets up
on the wrong side
of his
web.

     ***

<169>

Peter Parker
picked a peck of
something
radioactive,
so they say.

they? You know —
the guys
with the thought clouds.

***

He wanted to join
the Fantastic Four,
but they wouldn't trust
an odd number.
Superstition, they said
(as they knocked on wood).

***

An example
of comic book
censorship:

they couldn't say
his wrist device
"ejaculated"
webbing.

***

<170>

No one believes
his favorite song
is "Up, Up and Away" —
that is,
until you cite its author:
Jimmy Webb.

***

He watched the play
Kiss of the Spider Woman
while hanging from
the chandelier
above the audience.

His upside down
perspective
was not what caused
his discomfort.

***

His orphan status
proved pivotal
to his world view.

His philosophy
was based primarily
on the wise teachings
of his Uncle Ben —

no relation
to the rice tycoon.

<171>

***

Bungee jumping
de-mystified him
for a lot of people;

suddenly nobody
was impressed
anymore
when he'd go
swinging
from one building
to another.

***

The thrill-seekers
chase after only
feeling;

range and choice
of location, and precision
in your destination
make the difference
if your life
is not
the only one
at risk.

(Plus, en route
he gets to
peek
in people's
windows).

<172>

***

The superhero support group
wasn't only
his idea;
everybody thinks it is
because of his
neurotic reputation.

He agrees
it fills a need,
though there were those
who'd ridiculed it —
notably
Hulk and
The Thing.

Ironic that they'd be
the ones to shock the group
by breaking down
and crying in
each other's arms.

It wasn't pretty.

                ***

So, he wonders —
do you tell
your only living
relative
your true
identity?

<173>

He asks his buddy
Batman.
Batman puts him
on hold, then puts
Robin
on the phone.

Robin is
the more "out"
partner.

<174>

AN ANECDOTE FROM SHOWBIZ JOURNALISM

Once I interviewed
an actress/ singer/ model
who wore shades
and a full-body, tight
gray leotard, which had a hood
that also hid her hair.
As we chatted,
I could see her nipples, but
I couldn't see her eyes.
She seemed
quite high
on something.

We sat in a dim club
where she would sing
later that night.
The place would be
packed by then.
She'd be carried in
on a Cleopatra-style sedan chair
by some nearly naked boys;
she'd be
nearly naked herself. Nonetheless,
a smoke machine
would cast a fog around her.

I asked
if her father, a minister,
approved of her showbiz career.

<175>

She told me
that he'd just broken his leg,
and had to wear a cast —
she thought he looked so funny!
Then she laughed/shrieked wildly
and long. My glasses
were transparent, but,
with hers so dark, she couldn't see
my eyes. It struck me
as a tad ironic
that her name was "Grace."

Then someone officious
appeared, to dismiss me;
it was time "to run through something,"
so he said. Clearly, they regarded
the 10-minute interview
as a big favor
to a little newspaper.
It was 4 PM —
early for them, I guessed.

Now, I would go
back to my well-lit office,
and attempt to craft
some sort of article
from a few facts
and a lot of fog.
I had a headache
wearing shades
would never soothe.

<176>

PITCHMAN

in memory of Billy Mays, 1958—2009

Burly and bearded, shirt sleeves
half rolled up, he holds up his product
and barks at the camera
in a voice pitched higher than you would expect.
His tenor's not the lone surprise.

It seems he's always selling something different:
super strong adhesive,
putty that seals leaks,
a wash that smells like oranges
but cuts through years of crud
when rubbed on any surface.

He looks like a bear
and sounds like a songbird, albeit
a loud one; his smile
is so white, it could blind you —
anyway, you just can't help
but trust him. You thank God
he doesn't sell religion.

You hear there's a fan club
of gay men who wish
he would bed them, but he's faithful
to his lucky wife.

<177>

You see him on the tube
practically every day
for decades.
When you hear
that he's died suddenly,
you feel a pang.

You wish you had opened
your wallet,
and not just your heart.

<178>

PUPPET

They call him
"Dummy" —
carved from
clacking wood,
needing a human hand
shoved up
his back
to sit erect
and talk
in someone else's
voice. Even
his personality
is someone else's
so-called
"character" —
the mouthy creep
his owner
won't dare
be, except onstage,
hiding behind him.

But when slumped lifeless
on a straight-backed chair,
at last
he tells his own
cold truth:

behind his eyes,
dead trees,
dreaming of
leaves.

<179>

THAT EVENING SUN

DECADES LATER,
FOR MY LATE FRIEND STEVE

All these years after your death,
I'm told
that everyone knew
how I felt about you,
though I never breathed a word
to anyone, not even you —
everybody
in the class we took together
chronically;
even your lover Bob,
apparently, those nights
I slept on your couch,
way too drunk
to go home. He knew
that I was drowning
and was kind to me,
and made no confrontation.

Years later,
when I had a lover
of my own,
you reappeared,
and newly single;
you brought poems
and photographs
that found their way
into the paper
where I worked.
You worked
at the drugstore

<183>

at 15th & Spruce.
I'd stop by
to say "Hi,"
and have a soda; we'd both
keep it light.

I would hear
that you were dead
before I even had a clue
that you were sick.
It was so sudden
in those days, the "new disease"
nobody really understood yet —
swooping down
the way a hawk would
on a squirrel.

I'd no longer looked at you
as I once had;
I'd still had no idea
that you knew.
You must have —
everybody else did,
so they told me.

I wonder,
when you came
to reconnect,
if you hoped
that I might still be free.
I wonder
if you didn't know
that you were ill yet.
I wonder

<184>

if I dodged
a bullet.

And I wonder,
if I had been free,
and you had known
and told me,
if the knowledge
would have stopped us —
old friends
just crazy enough
to die for love.

<185>

PROSTATE CHECK

My urologist flicks out the lights
and shines a flashlight
through my sac.
"See the way it lights up
like a Halloween pumpkin?" he asks,
cheerfully oblivious,
apparently, to how my belly
blocks it from my view.

He kneels before me; gently —
mostly —
feels my balls;
makes me bend over;
shoves a finger
up my butt.

It is as intimate
as I have been
with anyone
of late.

No surgery
this year,
he reassures me —
not this new year
in my old age.

<186>

SALLY

Sour-faced Sally was
a scary-looking hard-ass
who dressed like
a businessman, but swore
like a longshoreman;
a strange choice
to hire for sales, I thought.
Still, I liked her
at first; she could be funny
in her blunt, crass way.
But, as you got to know her,
her cold center
would become more palpable.

She'd read
some of the notebook
on my desk, she said to me one day,
as if that were her business.
Then she'd added with a sneer,
"You're nuts.
I feel sorry for you."
Never mind
what kind
of mental hygiene
it must take
to go through a co-worker's
private things.
Or being too illiterate
to grasp his poetry.

<187>

One night,
several months later,
with a bottle
of Jack Daniels
by her side,
she shot herself
in the head.
She didn't leave a note.

When they told me
she was dead,
I wept. I no longer
know why.
Why shed tears
over someone
who'd been cruel to me?

Perhaps it was
because I understood
that pain, that drive
to blow out the harsh lights.
But my crazy notebook
takes my bullets for me —
to this day,
all these decades later.

Sometimes I think
that you really do have to be crazy
to stay in this world.
And when I do,
I write it down,
and think again.

<188>

FOR ANOTHER DEAD FRIEND

Sadly, our last talk
was awkward.

I didn't know
how ill you were.
In fact, I didn't even know
that you *were* ill —
you hadn't told me,
And our contacts
for so long
were limited
to telephone,
now that we lived so far apart.
All I knew
was that you were angry with me —
with no real reason, so I thought.
I held it against you
silently, later wrote you
a polite note of response
without expressing
my real feelings,
never heard from you again —
and wrote you off
in my own head,
despite our three decades
of somewhat distant
friendship.

I learned you had passed
via telephone, too,
from a mutual acquaintance,

<189>

who told me as if it were
an afterthought, beginning
"oh, by the way…"
I couldn't make myself
believe it.
The next day,
your partner called —
clearly, while going down a list —
and gave me
all the details of your funeral.
There was no more denying it.
All I could say was,
"I'm so sorry."
There weren't words
for how sorry I was.

But I never made the service.
My own partner
was in the hospital,
and unexpectedly,
for something serious
but, thank the gods,
not fatal;
not like cancer,
which eats people
to slow death
relentlessly, inexorably,
like that anger,
like the words
we never say.

<190>

NO BODY REQUIRED TO REACH HERE

In memory of Alexandra Grilikhes

words, the body that's drawn from air by the movement of will
        —from "Watching The Dance" by Alexandra Grilikhes

My late friend's poem
still holds her energy:
I don't care what other poets say,
she's still present in a way
that many of them will no longer be
when nothing's left of *them*
except their poetry,

"Wasn't she a lesbian?"
they often ask,
as if that ever made
a difference —
these guys who never
would have had a chance in hell with her
no matter what she was.

She was, by the way,
beautiful —
and she still is,
now that her energy
is free to resonate,
no longer bordered
by a body

and yet bringing life
unending
to her words.

<191>

Relief at last
after living in fear;
after the days of
unknowing,
seeing your loved one
prone
with tubes hooked up
to him.

The doctors
and nurses
were kind,
reassuring,
and careful
to tell you
the risks.
You nodded,
kept your cool —
you didn't want
to rock the boat.
Your terror
was a quiet sea
you rode, and hoped
that only you
could feel (not wild,
true, but plenty deep enough
for drowning). But,

<192>

when the waiting ends,
they tell you
all is well.

You sit beside him
while he rests —
safe, still
sleeping —
and you breathe,
grateful
for your breath
as well as his.
You wonder
how you lived
for so long,
not taking
a breath;
how you could fail
to notice
you'd spent
that much time
not breathing.

<193>

You sleep upstairs
as you did all day yesterday,
and as you've done, so far,
all day today. You've had another episode
of illness;
fiery pain, a Friday night
in the ER,
waiting behind a long line
of assorted winter injuries,
laid on a gurney in a hall,
less than half-sheltered
by a paltry screen —
no rooms were left —
until they poked and prodded you
at 3 AM with bleary-eyed,
caffeine-wired bedside manner.
Yet you still want
to put off the surgery
that could prevent
another reoccurrence.
I watch you hurt
and give what help I can,
give argumentative advice
until you listen,
take the medication
right, with milk
to kill the nausea;
but surgery's
another matter, one on which
you will not listen.

<194>

I am a hovering pest
without wings —
but one who, at least,
hovers
out of love.

Once you are home in bed
I hit the stores,
buy bland wet food
you will not eat,
cancel my plans
the moment I get home,
wait while you sleep
in case there's anything you need.
And find strange peace
in doing so, released
from endless self-preoccupation.
Outside, the wind howls angrily
as if to say, "Come out,
I want a crack at you."
But all I need
is safe in bed
and snoring reassuringly,
a droning sound
of constant comfort,
like the soft crash
of the tide
to those who live
not just beside the sea,
but by it.

<195>

GRIN AND BEAR

We argued in your truck
out on the road.
I can't remember
the subject, only
a welcome interruption:
as you flashed
your hot blue eyes at me,
a black bear came
scampering out of the woods
into our path, oblivious
to us as you, the driver,
were to him. I laid my hand
gently on your thigh. "Look,"
I said, in a quieter voice
than either of us had been using.

You did. You saw.
As if feeling
your eyes on him,
the bear looked up at us.
Startled, he jumped straight up
into midair, like some old
cartoon character — all four paws
left the ground at the same time.
He turned and scampered
back into the woods —
and that's
the only verb for it;
delicately, like a romping lamb.

<196>

We both
forgot our argument. We'd both known
that this area had bears, but neither of us
had seen one before.
We shared a grin, and drove on
in delighted silence.
I left my hand
where it was.

<197>

AN IMAGINED INTERACTION

And so I asked you,
"Can I touch your beard?"

You didn't answer,
but I took your look as "yes."

"It's soft,"
I said. "It looks
rough, but
it's so soft."

And then a kiss
dissolved a lot
of recent history.

<198>

SUPPORT

You sit with me before my surgery
and stroke my hand, and softly lend support;
Awhile without a word, yet you report
a wealth of subtle sentiments to me.
The nurse pops in, and says that the I.V.
may pinch me; I don't let my face contort,
wanting to seem brave and polite. We court
the best blood pressure with infused tranquility.
It's time to go. The doctor shakes your hand
as if we're at a sports event. I say
"I love you," as you do, with confidence.
They wheel me off. Though I wear no gold band,
I feel your presence near me when I fade.
I'll wake wrapped in your silent eloquence.

<199>

HOME

Now that it's quiet
here, and that
our times together
are, as well,
what holds me here
is not —
as I had hoped —
frantic desire, but
peace,
and the promise
of more.

The long journeys
we made in search
of something we
could not identify

have found their end
here in this calm,
where we fell into
family.

<200>

TO PEOPLE WHO COMPLAIN
THAT MY POEMS ARE "TOO DARK"

How dark
can anything be
that turns a light on
in your head,
no matter what
it lets you see?

<201>

INSPIRED BY LINES FROM THE
TAO TE CHING

*There is no greater misfortune
than having an enemy.*
—— *Tao Te Ching,* tr. Stephen Mitchell

He sees his former friend
on the corner, turns
to avoid him, takes
the longer way home.

Old betrayals
dog his every step,
though the sun shines
on this clear day.
The past
is a voice
in his head, louder
than the birds
chirping away,
the rustle
of the spring's
first leaves.

Out of sight
if not mind,
on the corner,
his former friend
stands still,
not thinking
of him.

<202>

UNSPENT

Sometimes exhaustion
is the only thing
you feel.

They call it being
"burned out" —
as if you were a house
after arson;

now empty of life
and the comforts
it carries, stripped down
to a shell,
all hollowed out.

And it's true,
you *do* feel like that.

But you still have
the capacity
to feel.

Unlike a knifed
Jack-o'-lantern,
whose flame
must be borrowed,

the light in your eyes
is your own.

<203>

CAT NAP

In memory of Suzie

Rest your face against
the black and white cat's
long, relaxing back,
stroke her soft belly,
bury your thoughts
in the purring and fur
as they surround,
suspend and supersede;
let go, drift off,
and dream yourself
a kitten in her womb,
and dream the world
a waiting ball of string.

<204>

CONSTANTINE CAVAFY

Openly gay poet and Classicist, 1863-1933

From all the things I did and said,
let no one try to find out who I was.
An obstacle was there, transforming
the actions and the manner of my life.
                    — Cavafy, *Hidden Things*

Cavafy was a wise man
and a kind man, who watched
other people struggle
with deep empathy.
He could easily imagine
how they saw
and what they felt, even
across long history. Even
the minds of the Gods
were no mystery to him.

Of his own heart,
we do not know
so much —
oh, we know
what he felt, if not
for whom; he had
devoted family and friends,
but kept his loves
"a secret life."

<205>

It was very brave of him,
back then, even
to tell us they existed,
and their gender.
The urge to know more
is a symptom
of our time, not his.

At the end, killed by an illness
he'd at first tried to deny,
he briefly raged
against the Greek Orthodox priest
who offered blessings
at his deathbed. Then he relented
and received communion.
Through his words,
he still communes
with us, whether
from Heaven
or Olympus.

<206>

TO A BUDDHIST FRIEND WHO WORKS WITH PRISONERS

for Jim Smith

This convict
says he wants
to see the ocean,
and it puts things in perspective.

He had asked you
what was your ambition;
you'd replied,
"attaining certain states
of consciousness,"
which sounds pretentious to you
now.

You can't ignore
the poignancy of people
whose mistakes
freeze them in amber;
maybe that
is what attracted you
to want
to work with inmates
to begin with.

Meditation only liberates
the mind. You come
to listen, and you're free
to leave. Hard to imagine
how life limits
those you try

<207>

to help. Now and then,
their statements
startle you, striking
an unexpected chord.

The Buddhist books
in which you found
your ethics
cite Samsara, the great ocean
of illusion.
Yet here a man
gives as his goal in life
his hope to see the ocean,
the mundane physical ocean —
with his eyes,
not with his mind.
You are stunned
by how that
humbles you.

<208>

THE MADONNA'S REVENGE

There have been several instances where statues of Christ in Catholic churches have been purported to bleed, and the Church has claimed some of them are authentic miracles. I think one thing the Church needs is a miracle that makes a statue of Mary bleed, but not from wounds.

The lady has had it;
had it
with healing the simpering sick,
with having to hold serene smiles
for breast-beating buffoons;
had it
with the boredom of enforced virginity,
with playing second fiddle to her
self-effacing son,
with twenty centuries of meaningless novenas
praising her subservience.
She's worn too long the heavy halo
of the uncomplaining, unpaid
live-in maid.
So, she begins
to bleed...
not from driven nails or thorny crowns,
not out of guilt,
not to atone for any actions not her own,
not as some mythic man-made martyr —
she bleeds
as a *woman*.
The sad blue gown, for centuries
her prison garb, is soaked through
with deep red.
The flow, held back
for all her unlived lifetimes,

<209>

pools around her proud bare feet.
Her breasts, too, swell
with sudden fullness,
nipples hard and heady with fresh milk —
but this time
there's no baby boy to suck her wellsprings dry;
this time,
the surge is pure pleasure.
Now the chapel air is wet with womanhood,
its smell
more rich and powerful
than any priest's pathetic little censer.
The worshippers are terrified, but can't
avert their eyes; her smile,
no longer trite, is now
triumphant.
The next time she appears to children, she will bring
a message on her own behalf,
a truer
testament.

<210>

The Queen of Heaven
stands with downcast eyes,
her statue placed
on a small pedestal
so, sitting, I can meet her gaze
straight on.

The serpent underneath her feet
seems to be smiling.

Cloaked in light blue —
the color of healing, some say;
some, the color of Spirit —
she carries her sadness
with dignity. This
is her secret.

Crescent moons cut
in the brass candle cup
cast long shadows
from a lily-scented votive.
Stray breaths
send them flickering
across her face.

Her eyes, painted on plaster,
wait to weep, unendingly —
yet seem to see, unnervingly,
unblinking.
I clasp my hands
and whisper Latin words

<211>

I do and do not
understand.

For a change,
far from guilt,
far from Church,
I lit this flame
of my own will.
I set the bowl of sea salt
at her feet, there in the North,
where things begin.

Mother of God? Perhaps —
but she is my mother
as well —
no matter who
may label me a sinner.

I have come here
to claim her love
as mine
by birthright,
and I feel the heat
of her belief
in me.

I bow my head.
I close my eyes.
She takes my hand.

We walk
among the lilies.

<212>

THIRTEEN O'CLOCK

We start counting over after twelve, we say,
because that's just the way
things are;
not, certainly, because we fear
the number that comes after it —
the proper number of a coven's members;
the number of apostles if — admit it —
Christ were following Himself;
the number of those Fridays that fall on us now and then,
when no one dares
to walk under a ladder
or break any such taboo;
the number of a certain floor
some taller buildings simply
refuse to acknowledge;
the number whose digits add up
to the quantity of elements that magically comprise
the universe
in metaphysical philosophy
that intellectuals deny;

the number whose existence *we* deny
as we insist
we're always starting over
rather
than just going on.

<213>

JACOB AND THE ANGEL

They tell you
Jacob wrestled
with an angel.

They don't tell you
it was erotic.

It lasted
all night.
It damaged Jacob's hip
and left him limping —

for no lover
desires to be forgotten,
whether human
or divine

It was significant
that the angel did not win.
There was no penetration —
only orgasm,
spontaneous
as rain,
also accompanied
by thunder
(though that noise did not wake
Jacob's wives).

And yes,
the angel blessed him as requested,
but would not tell him
its name, claiming

<214>

its name was the same
as that of the place
where they had grappled
all night long;

and he gave Jacob
also a new name;
also the name of a place;

as if to say
that where you stand
is who you are;

and he left Jacob,
now called Israel,
to wake lost
in the ruins
of their love,
knowing the man

would say that it
was just a battle,
not admitting
to the kisses
that transformed him,
claiming rather
that he'd triumphed
over God, not telling anyone

that God is what you love
in other men, and also
what they love
in you.

<215>

ABOUT THE ANGELS

Long ago,
before the New Age vogue for them,
I heard a bearded poet
in a battered leather jacket
say he "had a thing for them";
he loved the marble statues of them,
sad and solemn,
posed forever among tombstones
in the old Louisiana cemeteries.

More recently, I heard
the spoiled young daughter
of a well-to-do churchgoer
say she "hated" them;
anyone who'd own an image of one
had no taste. She looked smug
in this judgment.

When I was younger
and more literal,
I pictured them
with feathers; they were men
whose shoulders sprouted
giant pigeon wings — no, gull wings,
all white, made
of bone and muscle, and yet
giving off faint light.
I wondered if their movement made a sound
Like that of birds.

Now that I have seen them,
I know better

<216>

than to try to fit their likeness
into words.
All I know
is that you only call on them
when you are really desperate,
and that the sight of them
will turn a young man grey,
and that the shattering vibrations
one feels when drenched in their presence
leave you deeply shaken,
and forever chastened.

<217>

ENTER THE BEAUTIFUL

Enter the
beautiful;
bearded, magnificent
windows.

Enter
the beautiful;
enter the men
who were strangers.

Enter
the beautiful,
enter
the future where
light lives in ashes
half-hidden, where baskets
hold hands.

Enter
the beautiful,
breasts
bright with something
like sweat,
but less solid,
more mystic.

<218>

Enter
the beautiful,
rain
painting outlines
on all the invisible people
whose presence
you always
suspected.

Enter
the house
with no windows
because of
no walls.

Enter
the essence
of windows,
the essence
of beards,
the sweet odor of
sweat, the sweet odor of
light;

Enter
the lips

of the wizard,
the mountain
of minutes.

<219>

Enter
the beautiful,
enter
the forest

of genitals,
empty jails,
absences

birthing wild
birds, wild birds born
with ideas.

Enter
the blood-tub
where age
is misplaced,
where the photographs
dance
with abandon.

Enter
the beautiful,
enter
the ugliness
finding rare glimmers
in mirrors.

<220>

Enter
the beautiful,
be
entered by it,
be
burned till you are
something burning,
be
filled

with the forest,
the entrance,
the dance

that begins
and begins ...

<221>

ABOUT THE POET

A 2010 nominee for a Pushcart Prize, Jack Veasey is a Philadelphia native who has been living in Hummelstown, PA for over 20 years. He is the author of eleven previous published collections of poetry, most recently *Shapely: Selected Formal Poems* (The Poet's Press, Providence, RI 2013).

His poems have also appeared in many periodicals including *Christopher Street, The Pittsburgh Quarterly, Assaracus, Harbinger: A Journal of Social Ecology, The Philadelphia Daily News, The Painted Bride Quarterly, Fledgling Rag, Oxalis, The Blue Guitar, Bone and Flesh, Zone: A Feminist Journal for Women and Men, Film Library Quarterly (Museum of Modern Art, NYC), Experimental Forest, Tabula Rasa, Wild Onions, Mouth of the Dragon, Asphodel, Insight, The Irish Edition, The Harrisburg Patriot-News, The Harrisburg Review, The Princeton Spectrum, The Little Word Machine (U.K.),* and *The Body Politic (Canada),* among others. His poems have also appeared in a number of anthologies, including *Common Wealth: Contemporary Poets On Pennsylvania* (Penn State University Press), *Sweet Jesus: Poems About The Ultimate Icon* (Anthology Press, Los Angeles), and *A Loving Testimony: Remembering Loved Ones Lost to AIDS* (The Crossing Press, Freedom, CA).

His plays have been produced by Theater Center Philadelphia and Theater of the Seventh Sister (Lancaster, PA). He has hosted literary radio programs for WITF FM in Harrisburg and WXPN FM in Philadelphia. He was awarded a Fellowship from the PA Council On The Arts and is a two-time honoree of The PA Center For The Book's PENNBOOK celebration. For many years he hosted poetry readings in the Harrisburg area at The Art Association of Harrisburg's Paper Sword series and at Encore Books and Music, Borders Books and Music, and Open Stage of Harrisburg, and also taught poetry writing courses at Harrisburg Area Community College Community Education Center, Martin Memorial Library in York, and for the Dauphin County Library System. He is a member of Harrisburg's notorious (Almost) Uptown Poetry Cartel.

Veasey spent the seventies and eighties working as a journalist for such publications as *The Philadelphia Inquirer, Philadelphia Magazine, Pennsylvania Magazine, APPRISE, The Philadelphia City Paper,* and *The Cherry Hill Courier Post,* and editing a number of periodicals in Philadelphia and New York, including *The South St. Star, The Philadelphia Gay News,* and *FirstHand Magazine.* His articles for the *Philadelphia Gay News* won two awards from the national Lesbian And Gay Press Association. He recently wrote an article on Walt Whitman's relationship with his longtime companion Peter Doyle that was syndicated to 40 periodicals nationwide by the Gay History Project, followed by another article about Whitman's involvement in the United States Civil War.

<223>

A singer as well as a poet, Veasey has released one CD album of original songs, "Build A Fire," as lead singer of the folk-rock duo Open Book. In 2010, Veasey released a CD single of another original song, "Whether Or Not The World Knows." He formerly sang second tenor with the Harrisburg Gay Men's Chorus. He has been with his partner in life, David Walker, since 1978.

<224>

ACKNOWLEDGMENTS

Poems in this collection have appeared previously in the following publications and anthologies: *Assaracus, Below The Belt. Vol. 3: Erotic Poetry By Men* (Poem Sugar Press, Ed. Carla Christopher, 2014), *Celtic And Queer: The Irish LGBT Experience* (Squares And Rebels Press, Ed. Wes Koster, 2013), *Christopher Street, Fledgling Rag, Fox Chase Review, Gay Roots* (Gay Sunshine Press, ed. Winston Leyland), *Half Life* (Red Pagoda Press pamphlet, Ed. Craig Czury), *Heat, Mouth of the Dragon, Philadelphia Gay News, Poet's Tour of Harrisburg* (Good Sport Press), *Son of The Male Muse* (The Crossing Press, Ed. Ian Young), *The South St. Star, Sweet Jesus: Poems About the Ultimate Icon* (Anthology Press, Eds. Denise Duhamel & Nick Carbo), *The Truth of Blue* (Wit's End Press, Ed. David Walker), *Wild Onions,* and *Zone: A Feminist Quarterly For Women And Men.*

The poem "A Man Marries His Tan" has undergone radical revision since its original 1970s appearance in the magazine *Mouth of the Dragon.* Aside from its premise and its title, it now has little in common with the first published version.

<225>

ABOUT THIS BOOK

This book was typeset in Adobe Garamond Pro, a modern adaptation of a classic letterpress font. Modern Garamond faces are based on the work of Claude Garamont (c. 1480-1561), and italic designs by Robert Granjon. Adobe's OpenType version of this font was released in 2000. Poem titles and section titles were set in Franklin Gothic, a type family created in 1902 by Morris Fuller Benton. Widely used for headlines in the hot metal era, the typeface was neglected for many decades in favor of newer sans-serif headline faces. Several additional faces, including Alternate Gothic, were added to the Franklin Gothic family to make it more versatile for headline design. Franklin Gothic's clean, modern look has led to its use as official or logo type for New York University and the Museum of Modern Art.

The cover art is one of the oldest known paintings of a dancing male figure, from the Tomb of the Triclinium, near Tarquinia, Italy, circa 470 BCE.

<226>